. . . hearts go home
for the holidays

A Collection of Holiday Recipes

from
Heirlooms by Radford
Lincolnton, Georgia

Compiled by

Carole Miller Radford
for
Heirlooms by Radford

Copyright © 1994 by Heirlooms by Radford

ISBN 1-886300-00-3

First Printing - June, 1994
Second Printing - October, 1994
Third Printing - January, 1995
Fourth Printing - November, 1995
Fifth Printing - March, 1997

Printed in the USA by

WIMMER
The Wimmer Companies, Inc.
Memphis

Heartfelt thanks to my family and friends for contributing recipes which made . . . hearts go home for the holidays and Hospitality Southern Style very special cookbooks.

The Cover:
Pictured on the cover is the home in Metasville, Georgia, near Lincolnton, of my late grandparents, Mr. and Mrs. Glen McCurry. Though they are gone, the house still stands and happy memories fill the hearts of their family and friends.

My niece, Amy Wilkins Johnson, sketched the house for Christmas cards that my sister, Betty Miller Wilkins and I gave as gifts to "the twelve" at one of our McCurry Christmas Gatherings.

SAD RECIPE

I didn't have potatoes,
So I substituted rice.
I didn't have paprika,
So I used another spice.
I didn't have tomato sauce,
So I used tomato paste.
A whole can, not a half can,
I don't believe in waste.
A friend gave me this recipe,
She said you couldn't beat it.
There must be something wrong with her,
I couldn't even eat it!

. . . Over the river and through the woods to Grandma's house we go . . .

Everyone has cherished memories of holidays spent surrounded by family and friends. Holiday decorations, tables and sideboards laden with wonderful food. The sounds of laughter and music blended with happy conversation. The delightful smell of freshly baked bread, cakes, pies, barbecue or country ham. The taste of ice cold lemonade, eggnog or hot apple cider. The big bear hugs given in greeting and departing. Every sense that one has can recall such memories. No matter where life finds you on any holiday, your heart can always go "home".

This collection of recipes began with memories of my Grandmother Mattie Maude McCurry's house (pictured on the cover) where her twelve children (one of whom was my Mother, Beatrice McCurry Miller) and literally dozens of grandchildren and other relatives gathered for many holidays throughout the years.

For additional taste tempting southern recipes to consider in your holiday planning, see our cookbook titled "Hospitality Southern Style".

I hope you will enjoy the recipes in both books as much as I have enjoyed putting them together for you.

Carole Miller Radford

♥ · ♥ · ♥ · ♥ · ♥ · ♥ · ♥ · ♥ · ♥

Cookbooks, like history books, are but records of past experiences and recipes are like little heirlooms passed down through the generations of a family.

This book is dedicated to the memory of my Grandmother, Nannie, and my Mother, whose grandchildren called her Nana, and to the grandmothers and mothers that you remember.

HOUSEHOLD HINTS

--Hang baskets on inside of pantry door. Handy to use but out of the way.

--Keep several needles threaded with basic colors of thread and stick in a pin cushion.

--Keep your warranties and service manuals in one place.

--Organize your closet. Hang shirts, blouses, slacks, and dresses in color coded groups. Do same with shoes and hand-bags.

--To organize your sheets and pillow cases, first fold flat sheet into 12"x2' rectangle; fold matching fitted sheet in 1' square; place on left side of folded fitted sheet. Place folded matching pillow cases on top of folded fitted sheet. Fold right side of flat sheet over top. Put them in your linen closet. When you're ready to change your bed linens, just reach in and everything you need is folded together. You'll wonder why you never thought of doing this before. It makes life a little easier.

--Color code your linen closet. Place all the towels and bath cloths of one color together. You may want to have them in color coded stacks: towel, hand towel, bath cloth. Your linen closet will stay so much straighter.

--A good storage idea for ear rings is to place 4 to 5 plastic ice trays in your dresser drawer. Each cube section is perfect for a pair of ear rings.

--Peanut butter will get ink or grease off vinyl flooring. It will also remove paper labels on glass or plastic.

CANDY MAKING CHART

See Page 184

COOKING HINTS

To assist you while preparing your meals, you will find cooking hints throughout the remainder of this book.

Table of Contents

Anell⁵ ▷

🖋 3. 12

NEW YEAR'S DAY

ST. VALENTINE'S DAY

ST. PATRICK'S DAY

EASTER

4TH OF JULY

HALLOWEEN

THANKSGIVING

CHRISTMAS

. . . hearts go home for the holidays

New Year's Day

- PARTY FOODS -

CHEESE & BACON PINWHEELS

20 slices white bread (crusts trimmed)
1 can Eagle Brand milk
1/4 C. mustard
1 tsp. Worcestershire sauce

1 1/2 lb. sliced bacon
16 oz. shredded sharp
   Cheddar cheese

Roll each piece of bread flat with a rolling pin, wafer thin; set aside. In bowl, combine milk, mustard and Worcestershire sauce. Cut bacon slices in half. Lay 3 pieces of bacon side-by-side. Place bread on top. Spread the milk mixture. Sprinkle cheese on top. Roll up like jelly-roll and secure with toothpicks. Repeat until all bacon is used. Chill. Preheat oven to 375°. Bake for 30 minutes. Makes 5 dozen.

BACON WRAPPED WAFERS

16 slices bacon

16 Waverly wafers

Wrap 1 slice of bacon around each Waverly wafer, lengthwise. Place on broiler pan and bake at 250° for 2 hours.

A little light brown sugar may be rubbed on bacon for added flavor.

"WHAT'S IN THESE" CHEESE SNACKS

1/2 C. butter
1/2 lb. grated New York sharp cheese
1 C. plain (all-purpose) flour

1/2 env. onion soup mix
1/2 tsp. salt or seasoned salt

Allow butter and cheese to come to room temperature. Combine all ingredients. Roll into 3 or 4 rolls (about the circumference of a quarter or a dime for smaller crackers). Wrap in Saran wrap. Chill. Slice into 1/8" slices (approximately). Bake on ungreased cookie sheet at 375° for 10 to 12 minutes until edges are lightly browned. Yield: 72 to 75.

HAM & CHEESE ROUNDS

1 C. finely crushed potato chips
1/2 C. (2-oz.) shredded
   Cheddar cheese

2 (4 1/2-oz.) cans deviled ham
1 C. all-purpose flour
1/4 tsp. red pepper

Combine all ingredients; mix well. Shape mixture into a 9" long roll; chill well. Cut into 1/4" thick slices and place on lightly greased cookie sheet. Bake at 425° for 10 to 12 minutes. Cool on wire rack and store in an airtight container. Yield: About 3 dozen.

STUFFED MUSHROOMS

Fresh mushrooms
1 lg. can deviled ham
1/2 C. bread crumbs

Dash Tabasco
1/2 C. finely chopped mushroom
    stems

Use as many mushrooms as you plan to serve. Remove stems and wipe mushrooms inside and out with cloth dampened with lemon juice. Reserve stems. Mix deviled ham with bread crumbs, Tabasco and chopped mushroom stems. Fill mushroom caps and brush very lightly with olive oil. Bake on greased pan at 350° until mushrooms are softened slightly. Makes 24 stuffed mushrooms.

PARTY RYE CANAPES

36 1" bread rounds or party rye or
    pumpernickel
1 lg. onion, grated

1 C. mayonnaise
5 to 6 T. Parmesan cheese

Toast 1 side of bread. Spread the other side with onion. Mix mayonnaise and cheese. Place a small teaspoon of the cheese mixture over the onion. Broil 3 to 5 minutes.

A small olive hidden under the cheese provides a pungent surprise.

PIZZA SQUARES

2 cans crescent rolls
1 jar Ragu pizza sauce
1 C. grated mozzarella cheese

1 lb. browned ground beef
Seasoned salt

Spread 1 can crescent rolls in bottom of 9½x11" baking dish. Layer with meat, sauce and cheese. Top with other can of crescent rolls. Sprinkle with seasoned salt. Bake at 350° for about 20 minutes, until brown. Slice in 2" squares. Serve hot.

BARBECUED SAUSAGE BALLS

1 lb. hot pork sausage
    (Jimmy Dean brand)
1 egg, slightly beaten
1/3 C. dry bread crumbs (fine)

1/2 tsp. sage
1/2 C. catsup
1 T. white vinegar
1 T. soy sauce

Combine sausage, egg, bread crumbs and sage. Mix well and shape into walnut-size balls. Brown slowly on all sides in a heated skillet for 12 to 15 minutes. Drain off fat. Mix remaining ingredients and pour over sausage balls in skillet. Stir to coat several times. Serve hot in chafing dish with toothpicks.

. . . hearts go home for the holidays

CONFETTI DIP

1 pkg. Knorr's vegetable dip mix
1 10-oz. pkg. frozen chopped spinach,
   thawed and drained

1 can sliced water chestnuts, chopped
1 C. dairy sour cream
1 C. mayonnaise

Drain spinach (place thawed spinach in a plate, place another plate on top of spinach, squeeze plates together, tilt and drain water off spinach). Mix drained spinach with remaining ingredients; chill. Serve with assorted crackers.

COUNTRY HAM DIP

1 C. dairy sour cream
1/2 C. (packed) ground, cooked
   country cured ham

1/2 T. dry sherry
1/2 T. prepared mustard
1 T. chopped onion

Mix all ingredients. Cover and chill. Makes about 1 1/2 cups.
Serve with assorted crackers or on cocktail biscuits (see Table of Contents).

GALA DIP

Linda Holloway Cooper - Lincolnton, GA

8 oz. cream cheese
2 1/2 oz. chipped dried beef
2 T. minced onion
1/2 tsp. garlic salt

2 T. milk
1/2 C. sour cream
1/4 C. chopped green pepper

Mix ingredients well. Chill. Serve with assorted crackers or fruits.

HOT CRAB DIP

3 8-oz. pkg. cream cheese
2 8-oz. cans crab meat
1/2 C. mayonnaise
1/4 C. sauterne
1 clove garlic, minced

Lawry's salt, to taste
2 tsp. dry mustard
2 tsp. powdered sugar
A few drops onion juice

Combine all ingredients and refrigerate for 1 hour. Heat in 350° oven for 1/2 hour. Serve hot in chafing dish or in casserole on a warming tray. Serve with "dip" potato chips or Fritos. Fills a 2-quart casserole dish.

BAKED CAMEMBERT

1 8-oz. wheel Camembert cheese
1/2 C. chopped pecans

1 tsp. butter, melted

Remove top crust of cheese; top with pecans and butter. Bake at 375° for 14 to 18 minutes. Serve hot with crackers.

PATE MOLD

2 sticks butter
2 lg. onions, chopped
2 1/2 lb. chicken livers
4 hard-cooked eggs

1/4 C. cognac
1 tsp. salt
Pepper, to taste

Saute onion in 1/2 stick butter until tender. Remove from pan. Heat 3/4 stick butter in same pan. Add 1/2 chicken livers and saute on high heat 3 to 5 minutes. Remove. Repeat with butter and livers. Place 1/3 onion, 1/3 livers, 1 cut up egg and 1/3 cognac in blender. Blend at low speed, then on high until smooth. Repeat twice. Stir in salt and pepper. Place in prepared 1½-quart mold. Brush lightly and decorate with pimiento and green pepper strips.

SALMON LOG

1 16-oz. can salmon, drained
   (reserve 2 tsp. liquid)
2 T. minced onion
1 8-oz. pkg. cream cheese, softened

1/4 tsp. Liquid Smoke flavoring or
   1/2 tsp. Tabasco sauce
Chopped dried parsley flakes

Combine all ingredients except parsley. Mix well. Refrigerate for several hours, then shape into log about 8" in length. Roll in parsley flakes. Serve with assorted crackers.

VELVETINE SHRIMP SPREAD

1/2 lb. cooked and cooled shrimp,
   mashed with fork until minced

1/4 lb. soft butter
Salt, pepper and curry, to taste

Mix all ingredients. Chill.
Good on Melba rounds or any other cracker.

SMOKED TURKEY SPREAD

1 C. ground smoked turkey
3 T. mayonnaise
1 8-oz. pkg. cream cheese, softened

2 T. parsley, chopped
1/2 C. nuts, chopped

Combine first 3 ingredients. Shape into a ball or roll into a cylinder. Roll in nuts and parsley. Chill and serve with assorted crackers.

Wooden clothespins (with metal springs) are great for closing opened bags of potato chips, pretzels, etc.

Add 1/2 to 1 teaspoon baking powder to batter when frying fish. Makes batter light and crisp.

Thaw frozen fish in cold milk. This makes them flaky and fresh tasting.

- BEVERAGES -

AUNT JOANN'S OLD FASHIONED BOILED CUSTARD
(Base for Eggnog)
JoAnn McCurry Ferguson - Lincolnton, GA
(One of the Twelve)

1/2 gal. milk
6 egg yolks, beaten
6 egg whites, beaten stiff
2 C. granulated sugar

1/2 C. plain flour
6 oz. vanilla flavoring
1/2 pt. bourbon

Put milk in double boiler and heat. Remove 1 cup milk and beat with flour until smooth. Add back to double boiler. Beat egg yolks and sugar. Add to milk in double boiler. Cook until thick, then beat until smooth (by hand or with mixer). Add vanilla and cook over medium heat until mixture will coat a spoon. Refrigerate. When cold, fold in beaten egg whites until smooth.

Add 1/2 pint good "sipping" whiskey (bourbon) just before serving and stir. Serve in a punch bowl in a large bowl of ice.

Note: This recipe is over 100 years old.

REAL EGGNOG

12 eggs
1/8 tsp. salt
1 C. granulated sugar
2 tsp. vanilla
8 C. milk

4 C. whipping cream
1 C. bourbon
1 C. rum
Nutmeg

Place the eggs, sugar and salt in a mixing bowl and beat for 2 minutes. Place this mixture in a heavy saucepan over low heat. Stir and cook until mixture is thick enough to coat spoon. Remove from heat; cool for 15 minutes. While this cools, whip the cream until thick. Gradually add whipped cream, vanilla and milk to egg mixture. Add bourbon and rum last. Chill for 4 to 6 hours. Garnish with nutmeg. Makes 25 servings.

PARTY PUNCH

3 lg. cans unsweetened
    pineapple juice
3 C. orange juice
1 1/2 C. lemon juice
1/3 C. lime juice
1 C. fresh mint leaves

2 C. sugar (optional)
Ice block or ring
1 28-oz. bot. soda water
2 28-oz. bot. ginger ale
2 C. fresh strawberries,
    split into halves

Combine juices, sugar and mint leaves; chill for at least 2 hours. Strain or remove mint leaves. Place an ice block or large ice ring in punch bowl. Carefully pour ginger ale and soda water into bowl at the edge. Add strawberries and float orange or lemon and lime slices on top. Yield: 80 servings.

Note: Champagne may be added if desired.

- SOUPS -

CHARLESTON SHE CRAB SOUP

1 pt. milk
1/2 tsp. mace
2 sm. slices lemon peel or
   1 tsp. lemon zest
A few drops of onion juice
1 lb. white crab meat (fresh or canned)
1/2 stick butter

1 pt. cream or Half and Half
Salt and pepper, to taste
A few grains of cayenne pepper
2 T. bread crumbs
2 T. sherry
4 egg yolks, boiled, mashed fine
Parsley, to garnish

In a double boiler, heat milk, mace, lemon peel and onion juice. Simmer for 3 to 5 minutes. Stir in crab, butter and cream. Cook over medium/low heat for 12 to 14 minutes. Add cracker crumbs. Stir gently. Add salt, pepper and cayenne to taste. Cover; remove from heat and let stand 3 to 5 minutes. Add sherry just before serving. Place an equal amount of the egg yolk in bottom of each soup bowl. Pour hot soup over and garnish with sprigs of fresh parsley. Serves 6.

Note: If you can get she crabs with eggs, it makes the soup much more "authentic", however, this recipe tastes very close to the real thing.

COLONY HOUSE FRENCH ONION SOUP

4 lg. onions, thinly sliced
1/4 C. margarine, melted
3 (10 3/4-oz.) cans beef broth,
   undiluted
3 T. Worcestershire sauce

1/8 tsp. pepper
Salt, to taste
4 slices French bread, 3/4", toasted
4 slices Provolone cheese

Saute onion in butter in Dutch oven, over medium heat, until tender, stirring frequently. Add beef broth, Worcestershire sauce, pepper and salt. Bring to a boil. Reduce heat, cover and simmer 10 minutes. Ladle soup into individual wide mouth soup mugs. Top each with a slice of toasted bread. Top bread with a slice of cheese. Place under broiler (or microwave) until cheese melts. Serve immediately. Yield: 4 1/4 cups.

Note: Very nice when served in small heavy crockery soup bowls with handles.

Freeze leftover tomato sauce, beef or chicken broth in ice trays. Then pop them out into Ziploc freezer bags. They're great to have on hand for soups, stews, etc.

Use instant potato flakes to thicken soups, stews and gravy.

- SALADS -

GREEN BEAN SALAD

2 (15 1/2-oz.) cans whole
   green beans, drained
1 8-oz. bot. Italian dressing
3 med. tomatoes, peeled

1/2 lb. fresh spinach
Chopped parsley, for garnish
Grated Parmesan cheese (optional)

Place drained beans into large shallow dish. Pour Italian dressing over beans; refrigerate covered for 1 to 2 hours. Stir lightly every now and then to coat well. Peel tomatoes. Refrigerate until chilled. Wash and cut spinach into bite-size pieces. Drain beans (reserving dressing). Add a little of the dressing to the spinach leaves. Arrange spinach leaves on a large platter. Slice tomatoes in 1/4" thick slices and then halve each slice. Arrange the sliced tomatoes around the edge of the platter atop the spinach. Sprinkle on some of dressing. Mound beans in the center atop the spinach leaves. Sprinkle tomatoes with parsley. Add Parmesan cheese if you wish or serve it in a separate bowl. Makes 8 servings.

This is an attractive and tasty dish.

BLACK-EYED PEA SALAD

Sauce:
1/3 C. oil-packed sun-dried
   tomatoes, chopped
1 pkg. Sweet 'N Low
2 tsp. Dijon mustard

2 1/2 tsp. honey
3 T. red wine vinegar
1/3 C. olive oil

Mix all ingredients (3 to 4 hours ahead) in order listed. Pour in a cruet or covered bowl.

Salad:
1 10-oz. pkg. frozen
   black-eyed peas, cooked
1 sm. green pepper, diced fine
1/2 C. green onions, sliced
   (use tops too)
1 T. chopped pimiento

1 C. Monterey Jack cheese,
   in small cubes
1 bunch parsley, chopped (use tops
   only) or red leaf lettuce,
   cut in small pieces

Combine ingredients in order listed. Pour Sauce over salad just before serving.

MARINATED VEGETABLE SALAD

Wanda M. Holloway - Lincolnton, GA

1 bunch broccoli
1/2 head cauliflower
1 med. onion, sliced
1 bell pepper, sliced

1 lb. small mushrooms, sliced
1 T. dillweed
1 pt. Italian dressing

Prepare broccoli and cauliflower into flowerets. Add mushrooms, onions and bell pepper. Mix dillweed with salad dressing. Shake well to mix. Pour over vegetables. Marinate 6 to 8 hours in refrigerator. Serves 12.

PASTA SALAD

2 T. olive oil
1/2 C. diced carrots
1 sm. diced onion
1 T. parsley
1 C. ham or bacon, chopped
1 lb. ground veal or turkey

1 C. evaporated skim milk (added last)
1/4 C. white wine
6 fresh sage leaves or
   2 tsp. dried sage
Salt and pepper
8 oz. penne pasta

In a large skillet, saute carrots and onions in olive oil; add parsley, ham or bacon, and ground veal or turkey. Add white wine and simmer 45 minutes, stirring often. While this is cooking, boil pasta in salted water. Drain. Add evaporated milk to skillet; add salt and pepper to taste. Add sage leaves or dried sage. Stir in drained pasta and serve in shallow soup bowls immediately.

STUFFED SEASHELL SALAD

1/2 bx. (8-oz.) seashell macaroni
   (larger shells), cooked
   and drained
1/2 lb. Cheddar cheese, shredded
1 8-oz. pkg. cream cheese, softened
8 stuffed olives, chopped

1 10-oz. pkg. frozen English peas,
   thawed
3 green onions with tops, sliced
1 C. mayonnaise mixed with
   1 T. white vinegar

Cook and drain macaroni shells. Cool to touch. While macaroni is cooking and cooling, combine cheeses and olives to from a thick paste. Stuff each shell with pasta. Refrigerate until chilled. When ready to serve, mix with peas, onions and mayonnaise mixture. Serve on lettuce leaves. Serves 6 to 8.

. . . hearts go home for the holidays

- BREADS -

CHEESE BISCUITS

2 C. biscuit baking mix   2/3 C. milk
1/2 C. grated sharp Cheddar cheese

Combine biscuit mix and cheese in a bowl. Stir in milk with a fork to blend. Turn out on a floured board; knead gently 8 to 10 times. Pat out to 1/2" thickness and cut with 2" biscuit cutter. Place on ungreased cookie sheet. Bake at 450° for 10 to 15 minutes. Makes 1 dozen 2" biscuits.

COCKTAIL BISCUITS

1/2 C. softened butter or margarine   1 C. self-rising flour
1 3-oz. pkg. cream cheese, softened

Cream butter and cheese; add flour to make a soft dough. Roll on floured surface; cut with a small biscuit cutter. Bake at 350° for 12 minutes. Serve with country ham or other desired meats.

YEAST ROLLS
Wanda M. Holloway - Lincolnton, GA

2 pkg. yeast   1/2 C. Crisco shortening
1 1/4 C. warm water   1/2 C. granulated sugar
3 eggs, well beaten   2 tsp. salt
4 1/2 to 5 C. all-purpose flour   Butter
    (unsifted)

Dissolve yeast in 1/4 cup warm water. Let stand for 10 minutes. Mix in eggs, 2 1/2 cups flour, 1 cup warm water, shortening, sugar and salt in a large bowl. Beat for 2 minutes with wooden spoon. Stir in remaining flour to make soft dough. Cover; let rise for 1 hour and punch down. Refrigerate overnight. Three hours before baking, roll as desired. Let rise for 3 hours. Will double in size. Bake at 400° for 12 to 15 minutes. Makes 30 rolls.
    Make the day before.

To make pancakes brown easily, add 2 teaspoons cane syrup to batter.

- SIDE DISHES -

NEW YEAR'S BLACK-EYED PEAS
Beatrice McCurry Miller - Charleston, SC
(One of the Twelve)

1 16-oz. pkg. dried black-eyed peas
1 tsp. baking soda
1 ham hock

1 red pepper pod, broken into
   small pieces
1 lg. onion, peeled (stem end left on)
Salt, to taste

Pick over peas (remove broken peas or bits of trash). Soak in water to cover 2" over top for 3 hours or overnight or speed up soaking process by pouring boiling water over peas. Add baking soda. Cover and let stand. Drain peas (reserve liquid). Return liquid to pot; add ham hock. Boil 1/2 hour. Add peas, pepper, onion and salt. Cook slowly until peas are tender.

Eat a big helping for a healthy new year.

COLLARD GREENS

1 lg. bunch collard greens
1 ham hock
1 T. salt
1/2 C. sugar

2 tsp. Tabasco sauce
3 T. white wine
Water, to cover 1 1/2 to 2"

Wash collards in cold water. Remove tough stems with scissors. Cut leaves in bite-size pieces (using scissors you can cut several leaves at a time into pieces). Place water, ham hock and salt in a large pot. Bring to a boil. Add collards (a heaping handful at a time). When collards have cooked down some, sprinkle sugar, Tabasco and wine over them. Cover and simmer until collards are tender, but not mushy. Serve with hot pepper sauce made from hot peppers and hot vinegar. Makes 6 to 8 servings.

Traditional New Year's Day dish. Have a heaping helping so you'll have prosperity in the new year. Collard greens represent folding money.

GRITS SOUFFLE

2 C. cooked grits (as per
   (package directions)
1/2 tsp. salt

1/2 pt. Half and Half cream
1/2 stick butter
2 raw eggs, separated

Mix hot grits with cream until smooth. Add salt, butter and 2 well-beaten egg yolks. Cool. Beat the 2 egg whites until stiff and fold into grits mixture. Pour into a buttered baking dish. Bake at 350° for 30 to 40 minutes until brown on top. Serve immediately.

. . . hearts go home for the holidays

WHOLE BAKED SWEET POTATOES

8 med.-size, firm, raw sweet potatoes   **Salt**
Butter or bacon drippings

Wash potatoes and pat dry. Do not peel. Rub with butter; then rub with salt. Place on a baking sheet and bake at 350° for approximately 45 to 50 minutes or until potatoes are soft when mashed with your fingers using an oven mitt. Serve split open on top with a pat of butter.

So good and so easy!

Note: You can slice a stick of butter the night before and freeze in a single layer covered with wax paper. Draw the tines of a fork over top for design. Place in a pretty round glass dish 15 minutes before serving.

HOPPIN' JOHN
Beatrice McCurry Miller - Charleston, SC
(One of the Twelve)

2 C. raw, dried field peas
8 C. water
4 tsp. salt
1 sm. ham hock or 1/4 lb. hog jowl
2 C. long-grain rice (uncooked)

5 slices 1/4" thick hog jowl, fried crisp
and chopped (reserve drippings)
1 lg. onion, chopped
1 lg. pod dried red pepper, crushed or
1 tsp. dried red pepper flakes

Pick over peas; remove broken peas, etc. In a large pot, place peas, water, ham hock and salt. Cook over medium heat until tender. While peas are cooking, fry sliced hog jowl until crisp. Remove from pan. Chop. Brown chopped onion in bacon grease. In another large pot, place rice, using 1/2 pea liquid and 1/2 water to equal suggested amount of water for cooking 2 cups of rice. Place 2 cups cooked peas, bacon, drippings, onion and crushed red pepper pod. Cook, covered, over medium/low heat until rice is tender. Add more pea liquid, a little at a time, if rice gets too dry. Serves 16.

Note: Cut recipe ingredients in half to serve 8.

Traditional New Year's Day dish. Eat a hearty helping for good luck in the new year. A lovely low country tradition dating back to before the Civil War.

RICE AND MUSHROOM CASSEROLE

3 onions, sliced
2 C. mushrooms (fresh) or
2 4-oz. cans
1/4 lb. butter

1 can consomme
1 C. water
1 C. uncooked rice
Salt and pepper

Saute onions and sliced mushrooms in butter. Add consomme and water. Add rice and stir. Season. Bake in greased casserole dish, covered, in moderate 350° oven for 45 minutes to 1 hour.

- MAIN DISHES -

BASIL BAKED CHICKEN

1 broiler-fryer chicken, cut or quartered
   or 6 chicken breasts
1 8-oz. ctn. dairy sour cream
1 tsp. dried basil

1 pkg. dry onion soup mix
1 10-oz. can cream of mushroom soup
Chow mein noodles

Place chicken pieces in baking dish. Combine sour cream, basil and soups; pour over chicken. Top with chow mein noodles. Bake 2½ hours at 325°. Yield: 4 servings.
Double recipe to serve 8.

SHRIMP AND RICE AU GRATIN

1 1/2 T. butter
1 T. flour
1 1/2 C. milk
1/2 lb. sharp cheese
1/2 tsp. salt
1 tsp. curry

2 C. cooked shrimp
1 C. cooked rice
1 C. fine, soft bread crumbs
Dash paprika, Tabasco and
   Worcestershire sauce

Melt butter; add flour; blend well and add milk gradually. Cook until thick. Add 1/2 of cheese and cook until cheese is melted, stirring constantly. Add shrimp; mix with rice and cheese. Reserve a few shrimp for top layer. Place in buttered baking dish and sprinkle with remaining cheese. Add a dash of paprika. Bake at 350° for 15 minutes or until cheese is melted. Serves 6.
An old Charleston recipe.

SHRIMP WITH PEA PODS

3 T. oil
1/2 tsp. ginger
1 clove garlic, minced
3/4 lb. raw shrimp
1 6-oz. pkg. frozen pea pods
1/2 C. sliced bamboo shoots

1/4 C. chicken broth
1 T. soy sauce
1 tsp. sugar
1/2 C. sliced water chestnuts
Hot cooked rice

Heat oil in wok or frying pan; add ginger and garlic. Add shrimp and stir-fry for 1½ minutes. Add pea pods and bamboo shoots; stir-fry for 2 minutes. Add chicken broth, soy sauce, sugar and water chestnuts; stir-fry 2 minutes. Serve over hot fluffy rice. Yield: 2 servings.

Sprinkle a little salt in the pan when frying fish or other foods. It will keep the oil from splattering so much.

For tenderness, pour salted water over raw shrimp. Let stand for 5 minutes. Can be done with raw, shelled shrimp as well.

BEEF STROGANOFF

1/4 C. butter
1 lg. onion, diced
2 lb. top round steak, cubed or
    cut into strips
1 tsp. salt
1/4 tsp. pepper (freshly
    ground is best)
1 10-oz. can beef consomme
1/2 C. water

1/2 C. sherry
2 T. Worcestershire sauce
1 T. prepared horseradish
1/4 C. flour (plain)
1/4 C. water
2 4-oz. cans mushrooms
1 C. dairy sour cream
Cooked rice or noodles

Melt butter; saute onion. Remove onion and set aside. Add beef and brown on all sides. Add salt, pepper, consomme, water, sherry, Worcestershire sauce and horseradish. Cover and simmer for 2 to 2½ hours until steak is tender. Add flour blended with water. Stir in mushrooms and onions. Cook until thickened. Fold in sour cream. Serve over hot rice or buttered noodles. Yield: 8 servings.

This is a good company dish. Double the recipe for 16 servings.

HERBED HOLIDAY ROAST

2 tsp. salt
1 tsp. pepper
1 T. rosemary

3 1/2 to 8-lb. beef tip roast (cap off)
1 T. oil

Brown roast on all sides in a hot skillet in 1 tablespoon oil; then rub with rosemary, salt and pepper. Place roast on rack in open roasting pan. Do not add water. Do not cover. Roast in 325° (slow) oven to desired degree of doneness: 140° for rare; 160° for medium. For a 3 1/2 to 5-pound roast, allow 35 to 40 minutes per pound, depending on degree of doneness. For a 6 to 8-pound roast, allow 30 to 35 minutes per pound. For easier carving, allow roast to "stand" 15 to 20 minutes after removal from oven. Since roast usually continues to cook after removal from oven, it is best to remove it about 5° below the temperature desired. Yield: Four 3-ounce servings per pound.

LONDON BROIL

1 T. butter
2 med. onions, sliced
1/4 tsp. salt
2 T. oil
1 tsp. lemon juice

2 cloves garlic, crushed
1/2 tsp. salt
1/4 tsp. pepper
2 lb. flank steak or London broil

Melt butter; saute onions. Add 1/4 teaspoon salt. Keep warm over low heat. Combine oil, lemon juice, garlic, salt and pepper. Brush on top side of meat. Broil for 5 minutes; turn, brush with oil mixture and broil to desired degree. Slice thinly against the grain. Yield: 6 to 8 servings.

FRIED HOG JOWL (SLICED)
Beatrice McCurry Miller - Charleston, SC
(One of the Twelve)

**2 to 3 lb. hog jowl, sliced like
thick bacon**

1 heavy iron skillet (cast iron)

Trim rind from slices or have your butcher do it when he slices the hog jowl. In a heavy skillet (cast iron is best - the blacker the better), fry a few slices at a time until crisp. Drain on paper towels in serving plate. Keep hot in 150 to 200° oven until all of it is fried. Serve with Collard Greens, Hoppin' John, cornbread sticks and sweet potatoes (see Table of Contents). Serves 8 to 10.

Note: Serve on a large heated platter.

MUSTARD COATED PORK ROAST

**1 3-lb. pork roast (boneless or
cut of choice)
1 8-oz. jar mustard (any kind)**

**2 med. onions, thinly sliced
1 tsp. freshly ground pepper
1 T. white vinegar**

Preheat oven to 275°. Line a 9x13" casserole dish with heavy duty aluminum foil. Place roast (fat side up) in dish. Brush top and sides of roast with whole jar of mustard. Cover mustard with onion rings. Add pepper. Pour about an inch of water on bottom around roast; add vinegar to water. Bake uncovered 6 to 6½ hours at 275°. Don't be alarmed at how it looks; it will be black on the outside and wonderful tasting on the inside. Let cool a few minutes. Slice and serve. Makes 6 to 8 servings.

Double or triple recipe ingredients for a larger crowd.

SAUSAGE & GRITS CASSEROLE

**1 lb. sausage, cooked and drained
3 C. hot cooked grits
2 1/2 C. shredded Cheddar cheese**

**3 T. margarine
3 eggs, beaten
1 1/2 C. milk**

Spoon cooked sausage into greased 13x9x2" dish. Combine grits, cheese and margarine until melted. Combine eggs and milk. Add to grits mixture. Pour all over sausage. Bake at 350° for 1 hour.

Serve with hot, buttered, baking powder biscuits (see Table of Contents).

Note: Can be prepared at night, refrigerated and baked the next morning.

Good for "the morning after" New Year's Eve.

A 6 to 10 pound spiral-cut cooked ham is a great convenience. Refrigerate. Remove 30 to 45 minutes before serving. Serves 8 to 10.

. . . hearts go home for the holidays

SWEET-SOUR PORK

2 lb. lean pork tenderloin, cut in
   1/3" thick medallions,
   browned and drained

1 lg. can chunk pineapple, drained
1 sm. green pepper, cut in strips

Sauce:
4 T. brown sugar
2 T. cornstarch
1/2 tsp. salt
2 T. soy sauce
1/4 C. vinegar

1/4 C. water
1 C. pineapple juice (from
   can of pineapple chunks)
1 beef bouillon cube dissolved in
   1/4 C. hot water

Mix Sauce ingredients together and add to meat. Cook until thick and bubbling. Add pineapple and pepper. Serve over bed of rice.

MUSHROOM GRAVY

1 T. butter
1 T. olive oil
1/2 lb. fresh mushrooms, sliced
1/4 C. flour (do not sift)

1/4 C. dry white wine
2 C. chicken broth
1/4 tsp. ground black pepper
1/4 tsp. powdered sage

In a skillet, saute mushrooms in butter and oil. Stir in flour. Whisk until blended. Add remaining ingredients. Cook until thickened.

Good with poultry and as gravy for cornbread dressing.

- DESSERTS -

PARTY PIE

1/2 C. pecans
1/2 C. shredded coconut
1/2 C. semi-sweet chocolate chips

1 9" unbaked pie shell, partially baked
1 14-oz. can sweetened
   condensed milk

Layer the first 3 ingredients (in order listed) in pie shell. Pour condensed milk into the middle. Do not stir. Bake at 350° until bubbling and crust is lightly browned.

PEANUT BRITTLE

2 C. sugar (granulated)
1 tsp. soda
2 C. raw peanuts

1 C. water
1 C. Karo white syrup

Combine sugar, syrup and water in a heavy iron skillet. Cook over medium heat until mixture spins a "thread" when you pick up a little in a teaspoon and put it back in. Add peanuts and cook until your hear the peanuts popping. Stir constantly. Remove from heat; add soda, stir and spread quickly on a lightly buttered flat surface. When hardened, crack into pieces.

CREAMY FUDGE

1/3 C. butter
4 1/2 C. sugar
1 (14 1/2-oz.) can evaporated milk
1 C. marshmallow creme
1 13-oz. bar sweet chocolate

2 12-oz. pkg. semi-sweet
   chocolate chips
2 tsp. vanilla
2 C. chopped walnuts

Combine butter, sugar and milk in a saucepan. Bring to a boil and boil for 5½ minutes. Remove from heat; add remaining ingredients except nuts. Beat well. Add nuts. Spoon into buttered pan. Cool until firm. Cut into squares. Yield: 5 pounds.

GRAHAM CRACKER CRUNCH BARS

1/2 bx. honey graham crackers
1 stick butter or margarine
1 C. brown sugar (packed)

1 tsp. vanilla
1/2 tsp. ground cinnamon
1 C. finely chopped pecans

Separate each cracker into 4 sections and place on a foil-lined cookie sheet (with sides). In a saucepan, combine butter or margarine, sugar, vanilla and cinnamon. Cook for 5 minutes on medium/high heat, stirring all the while. Sprinkle nuts on each cracker section and pour cooked mixture on top. Bake for 10 minutes at 350°. Turn oven off and leave in the oven until cool. Store in airtight container. Averages 60 bars.

TOFFEE

2 C. rolled oats
1/3 C. melted butter
1/2 C. brown sugar
1/4 C. dark corn syrup
Pinch of salt

1 1/2 tsp. vanilla
1 C. semi-sweet chocolate chips,
   melted
1/4 C. chopped nuts

Thoroughly mix oats and butter; add brown sugar, corn syrup, salt and vanilla. Pack firmly into well-greased 8" pan. Bake at 450° for 12 minutes until dark brown. Cool completely. Loosen and turn pan over, tapping until candy comes out. Spread top with melted chocolate chips; sprinkle with nuts. Chill to harden chocolate. Cut into squares. Yield: 3 pounds.

CARAMEL FUDGE BROWNIES

1 14-oz. pkg. caramels
1/3 C. evaporated milk
1 pkg. German chocolate cake mix
1/3 C. evaporated milk

3/4 C. melted butter
1 C. chocolate chips
1/2 C. chopped nuts

Combine caramels and 1/3 cup evaporated milk in top of double boiler; melt caramels and keep warm. Combine cake mix, milk and butter. Place 1/2 of batter in greased 13x9" pan. Bake at 350° for 6 minutes. Sprinkle chocolate chips and nuts over top, then spread with warm caramel. Pour on remaining batter. Bake at 350° for 15 to 18 minutes. Cool before cutting. Yield: 2 dozen.

TURTLE CAKE SQUARES

1 bx. German chocolate cake mix
1 14-oz. bag Kraft caramels
1 stick margarine
1/3 C. milk

1 6-oz. pkg. chocolate chips
  (semi-sweet)
1/2 C. chopped pecans (or more)
Powdered sugar

Mix cake by directions on box. Pour half of batter into greased and floured 9x13" pan. Bake at 350° for 20 minutes. Meanwhile, melt caramels, milk and margarine together. Pour over cake while hot; top with chocolate chips and nuts. Pour remaining batter on top. Spread evenly. Bake at 250° for 30 minutes more. Cool and sprinkle with powdered sugar. Slice into squares.

AUNT WARDELL'S CARAMEL FLAN
Wardell McCurry Briceno - Jonesboro, GA
(One of the Twelve)

2 C. sugar
1/2 C. water
1 qt. milk

8 large eggs
1 tsp. vanilla
Pinch of salt

In a heavy saucepan over moderate heat, stir together 1 cup of the sugar and the 1/2 cup water until the sugar dissolves; continue cooking over moderate heat, without stirring, until golden brown. Pour the syrup into a round 10x2" cake pan (from a 3 to 4-tier cake set); tilt to coat bottom and sides; let cool for 30 minutes.

Heat the milk to lukewarm. In a large bowl, beat together until blended the eggs, remaining 1 cup sugar, vanilla, salt and 1 cup of the lukewarm milk; add the remaining lukewarm milk and beat to blend. Strain into the prepared pan. Place in the round 12x2" pan from the tiered set; add enough tap water to pan to come up about as high as the custard mixture. Bake in the preheated 350° oven until a knife inserted near the center comes out clean, about 50 minutes. Cool. Cover with Saran and chill.

Place a large shallow serving dish upside down over the flan; invert; remove the pan. There will be a generous amount of caramel syrup.

... hearts go home for the holidays

Valentine's Day

- PARTY FOODS -

CONFECTIONERY TREE
Betty Miller Wilkins - Prosperity, SC

1 12" styrofoam cone (white)
Dried white baby's breath or
   small dried flowers
Lace paper doilies (white)
Glue

1 2-lb. bx. assorted chocolates
   (caramel or Russell Stover
   soft centers)
Toothpicks
3 yd. white ribbon, 1/4" wide

Cover styrofoam cone with paper doilies. Stick toothpick in bottom side of candies and stick other end of toothpick 3/4" into cone, starting at bottom and working up. Top with a fluffy bow with streamers or with folded fans made from paper doilies wired to a florist pick; or, wire bunches of baby's breath to small florist picks and push picks into cone between candies. Use just enough to soften the look of the cone.

This idea is great for Valentine's candy and can also be made up with candies for Easter or miniature candy bars for Halloween. You may cover the cone with green foil and use ivy as the filler with strawberries.

DATES IN A BLANKET

1 bx. dried dates, pitted
Bacon (uncooked)

Toothpicks (wooden)

Wrap each date in a piece of bacon large enough to go around to be secured with a toothpick (one slice should wrap 4 to 6 dates). Bake on a cookie sheet with toothpicks pointed upward at 250° until bacon is done.

Unusual and good!

SPICED NUTS

1 1/2 lb. pecans
1 egg white
2 T. water
1/2 C. granulated sugar

1/2 tsp. salt
1/2 tsp. cinnamon
1/4 tsp. cloves
1/4 tsp. allspice

Beat egg white slightly with fork. Add the water. Then add the sugar, salt and spices. Stir until dissolved. Coat a few pecans at a time. Take out one at a time and place flat-side down on a well-buttered cookie sheet. Bake at 250° for 40 to 45 minutes. Cool a minute or so, then break apart. Store in airtight container.

MARK'S CHEESE BALL
Nancy Hurley - Hartwell, GA

1 8-oz. pkg. cream cheese, softened
1 jar pimiento cheese spread
1 jar Old English sharp cheese
1 T. Worcestershire sauce

1 tsp. onion powder
1/4 tsp. garlic powder
Dash Tabasco
1 C. ground nuts

Mix all ingredients, except the ground nuts. After thoroughly mixed, roll in ground nuts.
Very good!

"PLAINS SPECIAL"
Mrs. Jimmy Carter - Plains, GA

1 lb. grated cheese
1 C. chopped nuts
1 C. mayonnaise
1 sm. onion, grated

Black pepper, to taste
Dash cayenne
Strawberry preserves

Mix; mold with hands into desired shape. Place in refrigerator until chilled. When ready to serve, fill center with strawberry preserves. (Good also as cheese spread without preserves.) Serve with assorted crackers.
For Valentine's Day, mold in heart shape with hollow center or into a ring.

- BEVERAGES -

MAKE AHEAD CAPPUCCINO

For Each Serving:
2/3 C. milk
1 tsp. instant coffee
1 tsp. sugar

1/4 tsp. ghiradelli chocolate
Brandy, to taste
Whipped cream, flavored with brandy

Scald milk in saucepan. Add all ingredients except whipped cream and mix thoroughly. When ready to serve, reheat, beat with hand mixer; pour into cups and top with whipped cream.

Freeze tea or lemonade in ice trays. Fill tall glasses with cubes and then add tea or lemonade. You'll be amazed at how much better it will taste! This works the same with ice rings for punch; just freeze some of the punch in a ring ahead of time.

. . . hearts go home for the holidays

RED SATIN PUNCH

2 pt. cranberry juice, chilled
1 qt. apple juice, chilled

10 7-oz. bot. 7-Up cola, chilled

Ice Ring:
1 sm. bot. red cherries with
   juice, chilled

2 7-oz. bot. 7-Up cola, chilled
Ring or heart shaped mold

Combine Ice Ring ingredients and pour into mold. Freeze. When ready to serve, pour chilled juices first, then 7-Up over Ice Ring in punch bowl. Makes approximately 35 servings.

- SOUPS -

OKRA CREOLE

1 lb. cooked okra
1 onion, chopped
1/2 green pepper, sliced

Garlic clove, chopped
2 T. butter
1 C. strained tomatoes

Drain cooked okra. Brown onion, pepper, and garlic lightly in butter; add tomato and simmer 5 minutes. Add okra, reheat, serve hot.

FROZEN TOMATO FROST

5 C. tomato juice or tomato soup
2 celery stalks
1 T. chopped onion
1 tsp. salt
3 T. fresh lemon juice
1 tsp. grated lemon rind

1 T. sugar
Dash of pepper
1/4 tsp. curry powder
3/4 C. salad dressing or mayonnaise
Sour cream

Heat 2 cups tomato juice or soup with celery, onion, salt, lemon juice and rind, sugar, pepper, and curry powder. Bring to boil and simmer for 5 minutes. Strain mixture. Add salad dressing, beating with a rotary egg beater until very smooth. Stir in remaining tomato juice. Pour mixture into two ice-cube trays and freeze until firm. Scrape out portions to look like pink snow. Serve at once with teaspoon of sour cream on top. Makes 6 to 8 servings.

For a quick white sauce, melt 2 tablespoons butter in skillet; add 3 tablespoons sifted plain flour. Stir; add milk until consistency desired.

- SALADS -

MARINATED BEET SALAD

1 16-oz. can sliced beets, drained
1 T. beet liquid from can of beets
2 T. olive oil
2 T. cider vinegar
1/4 tsp. dried thyme, crushed fine

1/8 tsp. salt
1/8 tsp. pepper
Leafy green lettuce
1 red onion, thinly sliced into rings

Drain beets. Set aside. In a mixing bowl, combine beet liquid, olive oil, vinegar, thyme, salt and pepper. Add drained beet slices. Serve on leafy green lettuce; top with thinly sliced red onion rings.

BING CHERRY SALAD

1 can Bing cherries, drained
   (reserve juice)

2 sm. pkg. cherry Jell-O
1 C. cherry wine

Drain cherries and reserve juice. Measure water required to make the Jell-O; add water and cherry juice to the wine enough to make 3 cups of liquid total. Heat until just before boiling point. Pour over the Jell-O; mix well and add the cherries. Pour into large heart mold, individual heart or other shaped molds. Refrigerate until congealed.

Sauce:
1 4-oz. pkg. cream cheese, softened
1/4 C. nuts, finely chopped

Mayonnaise
1 tsp. sugar

Combine softened cream cheese, nuts, enough mayonnaise to thin and sugar. Mix well. Use a pastry bag to pipe it on top of unmolded salad in shape of heart.
   Note: A Ziploc bag with one bottom corner snipped off makes a good "pastry bag". Just place Sauce in the bag, twist and squeeze the Sauce out.

PINK PERFECTION SALAD

1 lg. can crushed pineapple, drained
1 can Comstock cherry pie filling

1 can Eagle Brand condensed milk
1 9-oz. ctn. Cool Whip, thawed

Mix and chill or freeze and cut into squares.
   Coconut, nuts, etc., may be added, if desired.
   Use a heart mold or individual heart molds, if desired.
   Note: Rub just a little mayonnaise inside mold before putting salad in. Unmolds easier.

SHRIMP SALAD

1 pkg. lemon gelatin
1 C. boiling water
1 C. Half and Half cream
1/2 C. mayonnaise or salad dressing
5 oz. glass pimiento cheese

1 (5 1/2-oz.) can shrimp (or more)
3 hard-cooked eggs, cut fine
1 T. grated onion
2 T. chopped green pepper

Mix gelatin and boiling water. Blend cream, mayonnaise and cheese; fold together. Add shrimp, eggs, onion and green pepper. Refrigerate until set.

SUE'S STRAWBERRY PRETZEL SALAD
Sue Goolsby Ashmore - Lincolnton, GA

2 C. crushed pretzels
4 T. sugar (granulated)
1 stick margarine, melted
1 8-oz. pkg. cream cheese, softened
1 med. ctn. Cool Whip, thawed
3/4 C. confectioner's sugar, sifted

1 6-oz. bx. strawberry Jell-O
2 C. boiling water
1/2 C. cold water
2 10-oz. pkg. Birds Eye
    frozen strawberries

Mix crushed pretzels, sugar, melted butter and press into bottom of a lightly greased 9x13" casserole dish. Bake for 10 minutes at 350°. Cool.

Meanwhile, mix softened cream cheese, thawed Cool Whip and sifted confectioner's sugar. Spread over cooled pretzel layer. Mix Jell-O with 2 cups boiling water until dissolved. Add cold water. Stir to blend. Refrigerate until partially set. Fold in frozen strawberries. Pour mixture over cream cheese mixture. Cover with plastic wrap and refrigerate until completely set, approximately 4 to 6 hours. Makes 10 to 12 servings.

SLICED TOMATO SALAD

6 lg. tomatoes, thickly sliced
Salt and freshly ground black pepper
1/4 C. scallions, finely chopped
2 T. fresh basil leaves, chopped or
    2 tsp. dried
1/4 C. wine vinegar

3/4 C. oil
1 clove garlic, finely chopped
1 tsp. Worcestershire sauce
2 tsp. salt
1/2 tsp. black pepper
1/2 tsp. sugar

Arrange layers of the tomato slices in an attractive serving dish; sprinkle each layer with salt and pepper to taste, scallions and basil. Combine the remaining ingredients in a bowl and beat with fork or wire whisk. Pour over the tomatoes and chill. Serves 8.

Quick Variation: Slice 3 to 4 large tomatoes 1/4" thick; arrange on platter overlapping slices slightly. Mix together 1/4 cup olive oil, 3 tablespoons wine vinegar and a pinch of sugar. Pour over tomatoes. Sprinkle with 2 teaspoons crumbled basil. Add salt and freshly ground black pepper. Cover with plastic wrap and refrigerate at least 1 hour before serving. Makes 8 servings.

Note: Really good in summer when tomatoes are in season.

- BREADS -

ROMANTIC FRENCH BREAD

1 loaf French bread, partially frozen,
    sliced 1" thick
Olive oil

Parmesan cheese, grated
Chives
Paprika

With a sharp knife, cut as large a heart as possible from each partially frozen slice of bread. (They don't have to exactly look alike.) Brush each heart with olive oil. Sprinkle with grated Parmesan cheese, a few chives and a dash of paprika over cheese. Bake at 325 to 350° until lightly browned and cheese has melted. Serve in heart-shaped bread basket.

STRAWBERRY BREAD & BUTTER

Bread:
1 1/2 C. plain flour
1 C. granulated sugar
1 1/2 tsp. ground cinnamon
1/2 tsp. salt
1/2 tsp. baking soda

2 eggs, beaten
1/2 C. vegetable oil
1 C. frozen strawberries,
    thawed and drained

Mix dry ingredients together. Mix eggs, oil and strawberries together. Add to dry ingredients. Bake in a 9x5" greased and floured loaf pan at 350° for 1 hour.

Strawberry Butter:
1 10-oz. pkg. frozen strawberries
1 C. soft butter

1 C. sifted powdered sugar

Combine ingredients. Mix with hand mixer. Spread on Strawberry Bread. Makes 2 1/2 cups.

Note: Strawberry Butter tastes wonderful on hot biscuits too!

VALENTINE FRENCH TOAST
Nancy Hurley - Hartwell, GA

6 white or whole-wheat bread slices
2 eggs
1/2 C. milk

1/4 tsp. salt
2 T. butter or margarine
Confectioner's sugar or currant jelly

Cut bread with heart-shaped cookie cutter. (Use trimmings later, for bread pudding.) In a medium bowl, with rotary beater, beat the eggs with the milk and salt just until well combined, but not frothy. Dip bread cutouts into egg mixture, coating both sides; shake off any excess. In hot butter in large skillet, saute the bread cutouts about 3 minutes on each side or until crisp and golden. Drain toast well on paper towels. Makes 3 servings.

To serve: Sprinkle lightly with confectioner's sugar. Place heart-shaped cinnamon candy in middle and/or around edges or half of strawberry, shaped like a heart or dab of strawberry jam in middle.

Any shaped cutouts can be used for other holidays. Change decorations accordingly.

HEART SHAPED CROUTONS

8 slices French bread　　　　　　**1 tsp. dried chives**
1/2 C. butter

Remove crusts from bread. Using a very small heart-shaped cookie cutter (or a sharp paring knife), cut bread in heart shapes. Melt butter; add chives. Place "hearts" in single layer on baking sheet. Brush all sides with melted butter. Bake at 250° for 1 hour or until lightly browned. Store in Ziploc bag. Use on salads or in soups.

- SIDE DISHES -

HARVARD BEETS

1 15-oz. can sliced beets, drained

Set beets aside. Make Sauce and pour over beets. Cool 1/2 hour. Just before serving, heat beets and sauce in 2 tablespoons butter.

Sauce:
1/2 C. sugar　　　　　　　　　　**1/2 T. cornstarch**
1/2 C. vinegar

Combine ingredients and bring to a boil. Boil for 5 minutes.
For Valentine's Day, cut beets into hearts with small cookie cutter.

CELERY AND ENGLISH PEA CASSEROLE

1 C. chopped celery　　　　　　　**2 T. chopped pimiento**
2 C. frozen green peas　　　　　　**1/2 C. toasted almonds**
1 can mushroom soup　　　　　　　**1 sm. can mushrooms**

Steam celery 10 minutes; steam frozen peas 7 minutes. Place peas, celery, mushrooms, pimientos and soup in alternate layers in buttered casserole dish. Top with toasted almonds. Place in 350° oven for 30 minutes.
Serve with toast points cut in heart shapes.

CHEESE-STUFFED PEARS

1 8-oz. pkg. cream cheese, softened　　**2 med.-size pears, peeled,**
1 T. milk or cream　　　　　　　　　　**halved and cored**
1/4 tsp. almond extract or to taste　　**2 T. slivered toasted almonds or**
1/2 C. chopped raisins　　　　　　　　**chopped nuts**

In small bowl of mixer, beat cheese, milk and extract until well blended and fluffy. Stir in raisins. Using ice cream scoop or 2 spoons, shape mixture in 4 balls; place on cut sides of pear halves. Sprinkle with almonds; serve at once. Serves 4.

GREEN BEAN CASSEROLE

1 can French-style green beans,
 drained
1 can cream of mushroom soup
 (undiluted)

1/2 can sliced water chestnuts*
1 can French-fried onion rings

*Cut with very small heart cookie cutters into hearts or cut with sharp knife into hearts.

Preheat oven to 325°. Combine green beans, soup and chestnut hearts in casserole dish. Bake until bubbly. Add onion rings. Bake 5 more minutes. Serve hot. Serves 4.

MUSHROOMS AND SOUR CREAM

1 lb. mushrooms
3 T. butter
2 T. water

1 C. sour cream
Salt and paprika, to taste

Wash mushrooms, and slice if desired. Place butter and water in skillet, and saute mushrooms gently. When tender (about 15 minutes), add sour cream. Cook slowly, stirring occasionally, until sauce is of desired consistency (about 10 minutes). Season with salt and paprika.

HEART SHAPED OVEN BAKED FRIES

4 to 6 lg. potatoes, peeled and sliced
 into 1/4" thick rounds, crossways
2 egg whites, beaten until frothy
Cajun seasoning, to taste

Salt, to taste
Vegetable spray
Small heart cookie cutter

Preheat oven to 400°. Cut each round of potato into a heart. Dip into egg whites. Sprinkle with seasonings to taste. Place on cookie sheet sprayed with vegetable spray in a single layer. Coat tops lightly with vegetable spray. Bake. Stir often until lightly browned and crisp.

Note: Sweet potatoes may be prepared the same way.

RED RICE

1 C. raw rice (Uncle Ben's)
3 strips bacon
1/4 C. chopped onion
1/4 C. chopped green pepper
 (optional)

3 C. canned tomatoes
1 T. sugar
1 tsp. salt
1/4 tsp. pepper
1/4 tsp. dried basil

Cook rice; set aside. Fry bacon until crisp, then crumble; set aside. Saute onions and green pepper in bacon drippings until onions are soft, but not browned. Add tomatoes, sugar, salt, pepper and basil. Add cooked rice. Pour into greased casserole dish. Bake for 30 minutes at 350°. Makes 8 servings.

TOMATO CREAM SAUERKRAUT

1 C. thick sour cream
1 sm. can tomato paste

1/2 C. brown sugar
1 (1-lb. 13-oz.) can sauerkraut

Blend sour cream, tomato paste, and sugar. Add sauerkraut and mix thoroughly. Bake in greased casserole dish in moderate 350° oven for 1/2 hour.

- MAIN DISHES -

CHICKEN PARMESAN

1 4-oz. pkg. saltine crackers,
    crushed into crumbs
3/4 C. grated Parmesan cheese

6 chicken breast halves,
    boneless, skinless*
1 stick melted butter

*12 boneless, skinless chicken thighs may be used in place of chicken breasts for this recipe.

Combine cracker crumbs and cheese. Dip chicken into butter, then roll in crumb mixture. Place on foil-lined baking sheet. Bake uncovered at 350° for 1 hour. Makes 6 servings.

CHICKEN WITH MARMALADE SAUCE

6 boneless, skinless chicken breast
    halves, trim any fat off
2 T. olive oil
1 tsp. seasoned salt
1/2 tsp. garlic salt

1/4 tsp. ground sage
1/4 tsp. pepper
1 T. dried cilantro or 2 T. fresh
    chopped cilantro or parsley

In a heavy skillet, place olive oil. Season chicken with seasoned salt, garlic salt, pepper, sage and cilantro. Brown chicken in olive oil on both sides. Leave chicken in skillet and top with sauce. Serves 6.

Sauce:
2 jars baby food peaches

3 T. orange marmalade

Mix and pour over chicken.

Olive oil, seasoned salt and tarragon mixed together are great to put on chicken while baking it.

HONEY LEMON CHICKEN

1/2 C. butter or margarine, melted
2 T. honey
1 T. chopped parsley
1 T. grated lemon rind
    (yellow part only)

1 1/2 tsp. seasoned salt
4 chicken breast halves,
    boneless and skinless
Strawberry preserves or fresh
    strawberries, for garnish

In a small bowl, mix butter, honey, parsley, grated lemon rind, and seasoned salt; blend well. Use one half of mixture to baste one side of each chicken breast. Broil 7 to 10 minutes on one side; turn and baste with remaining mixture. Broil for 7 to 10 minutes more or until done. Garnish with strawberry preserves or fresh strawberries. Makes 4 servings.

QUICK CHICKEN DIVAN

2 (6 1/2-oz.) cans white chicken,
    drained
2 pkg. frozen chopped broccoli,
    cooked
1 C. shredded sharp Cheddar cheese

1 can cream of mushroom soup
1/2 C. milk
2 C. herb seasoned stuffing mix
1/2 stick butter or margarine, melted
Paprika, for garnish

In a 9x13" casserole dish, layer (in order) chicken, broccoli, soup, milk and cheese. Top with stuffing mixed with melted butter. Bake at 350° for 20 minutes. Garnish with paprika.

BEEF BURGUNDY HEARTS

2 to 3 lb. ground round, seasoned
    to taste, shaped into 8 equal
    heart-shaped patties
1 pkg. dry onion soup mix
1 10-oz. can cream of celery soup

1 10-oz. can cream of mushroom soup
1 C. Burgundy wine
1 4-oz. can mushrooms
Hot buttered noodles, cooked

Place heart shaped patties in a casserole dish. Top with soups (dry and canned) and wine. Add mushrooms 30 minutes before serving. Bake at 350° for 1½ hours. Serve over hot, buttered noodles. Yield: 6 to 8 servings.

To make beef roasts, turkey or hen retain juices and tenderness. pat dry then brown on top of stove in skillet in just enough oil to keep from sticking. Turn often to brown evenly. Place on roasting rack, uncovered. Season and roast according to recipe.

. . . hearts go home for the holidays

STUFFED MEAT LOAF

2 lb. ground chuck or round
1 egg, beaten
2 cloves garlic, minced
1 C. bread crumbs
1 tsp. Worcestershire sauce
1/2 tsp. oregano
1/2 tsp. pepper

1 sm. onion, diced
3 T. butter
1/2 C. water
5 hard-boiled eggs, remove shells
1 sm. can tomato sauce
1/2 tsp. sugar
1/4 C. water

Combine first 10 ingredients and pat mixture out to form a rectangle about 2" thick. Place boiled eggs in middle (end to end -- cut a little of the white off to fit eggs together). Fold meat over (jelly-roll style). Place in baking dish. Combine tomato sauce, sugar and water. Pour over meat loaf. Bake at 350° for 1 hour. Slice.

Serving suggestion: Slice onto platter; surround slices with hot mashed potatoes topped with Cheddar cheese.

- DESSERTS -

RED VELVET CAKE

1 stick butter
1 1/2 C. sugar
2 eggs
1 C. buttermilk
2 oz. red cake coloring
2 T. cocoa

1 tsp. vanilla
1 tsp. vinegar
1 tsp. soda (sifted)
2 1/2 C. cake flour
1 tsp. salt

Cream butter, sugar and eggs. Make paste of cake coloring and cocoa. Add to mixture. Add salt to flour and sift. Add flour and buttermilk, alternately, mix well. Add vanilla; mix well. Add soda and vinegar and don't beat, just blend. Bake in three 9" layer pans about 30 minutes at 350°.

Icing:
2 tsp. cornstarch
1 C. water
1 C. sugar

2 sticks butter
1 tsp. vanilla
1/2 C. chopped pecans

Cook cornstarch and water until thick. Let cool. Cream sugar, butter and vanilla until fluffy. Add pecans. Add to cooled mixture; beat until it has the consistency of whipped cream.

GLAZED CHERRY PIE

1 9" unbaked pie shell
1/2 C. finely chopped
   blanched almonds
4 C. fresh pitted red cherries or
   2 (1-lb. 4-oz.) cans tart
   red cherries, drained
1 C. sugar
1/8 tsp. salt

1/4 C. flour
1 T. lemon juice
2 T. butter or margarine
3/4 C. red currant jelly
1/8 tsp. cloves
1/8 tsp. cinnamon
3/4 C. whipped cream (optional)

Sprinkle almonds over bottom of pie shell. Preheat oven to 375°. In large bowl, combine cherries, sugar, salt, flour and lemon juice. Pour into unbaked pie shell. Dot with butter; bake for 40 minutes. Cool pie on wire rack. Melt jelly in small saucepan. Stir in cloves and cinnamon. Spoon over cherries. Cool. If desired, serve topped with whipped cream. Makes 6 to 8 servings.

CHOCOLATE COVERED ALMONDS

1/8 tsp. vanilla
2/3 C. semi-sweet chocolate bits

2 C. whole roasted almonds

Melt chocolate in top of double boiler over hot, not boiling, water, stirring frequently. When chocolate is melted, reduce heat. Add vanilla. Dip almonds into chocolate with a fork, remove and place on wax paper to cool. When chocolate has hardened, store in airtight container. Yield: 2 cups.

Note: Roasted pecan halves may be substituted for almonds.

MARZIPAN STRAWBERRIES OR HEARTS

1 recipe Marzipan (see Table of
   Contents - Easter: Desserts)
Blanched almonds, slivered
Green food coloring

2 tsp. water
Red decorator's sugar or
   1 T. strawberry Jeli-O mixed
   with 1 T. sugar

For strawberries: Shape Marzipan in shape of strawberries (roll between palms of hands and shape with fingers -- it's really like playing with play dough). Roll Marzipan strawberries in red sugar. Roll stem end in green sugar. Soak slivered almonds in green food coloring. Drain on paper towels. Stick in stem end of strawberry for stem.

For hearts: Shape Marzipan into small hearts (or roll it out and cut small hearts). Coat with red decorator's sugar.

. . . hearts go home for the holidays

ROSALYN'S MOCK STRAWBERRIES

Rosalyn Adams - Washington, GA

Make 3 to 5 days before serving.

1 C. Angel Flake coconut
1 14-oz. can Eagle Brand
   sweetened condensed milk
1 C. pecans, finely chopped
3 sm. pkg. strawberry Jell-O
2 or 3 drops red food coloring

Red decorators sugar
Green decorators sugar
Slivered almonds
2 drops green food coloring
1 tsp. water

Mix all ingredients together in a bowl. Cover and refrigerate for 3 to 5 days. Then form into strawberry shapes. Roll in red decorators sugar, roll stem end in green decorators sugar. Put slivered almonds in green food coloring to coat; drain on paper towels. Stick 1 in each stem end; place strawberries on wax paper and refrigerate until ready to serve. Makes approximately 6 dozen.

Note: If you don't have slivered almonds, color toothpicks with green food coloring, cut in half and use for stems.

You may buy decorators sugar or make it yourself by putting granulated sugar in a jar, add a drop or two of food coloring and shake or mix with a fork.

VALENTINE KISSES

2 C. powdered dry milk
1 C. peanut butter (smooth or crunchy)

1 1/2 C. honey
1 1/4 C. coconut

In a large bowl, combine dry milk, peanut butter and honey until soft dough forms. Roll into 3/4" balls; roll in coconut. Makes 2 dozen.

CANDY COATED COOKIE HEARTS

1 (1 1/2-lb.) pkg. vanilla or
   chocolate candy coating
1 T. Crisco

60 small heart-shaped cookies
   (purchased or baked)*

*See Table of Contents for Versatile Sugar Cookie recipe. Christmas: Desserts.

Following package directions, melt chocolate or vanilla candy coating; dip each cookie in mixture to coat. Place on wax paper until coating firms. Store in airtight container.

HEART TARTS

1 1/2 C. (3 sticks) butter, softened
3/4 C. plus 1 T. confectioner's
   (10X) sugar
1 egg, beaten

2 C. all-purpose flour
1 C. cornstarch
2 C. finely ground pecans
5 T. seedless raspberry jam

Mix butter and 3/4 cup 10X sugar in bowl until light and fluffy. Beat in egg. Add flour, cornstarch and pecans; mix well. Refrigerate, wrapped, overnight. Roll out about half the dough on lightly floured surface to 1/8" thickness. Cut out 32 hearts with 3" heart-shaped cookie cutter. Cut smaller heart out of centers with 1" heart cookie cutter. Cut out 32 solid hearts with 3" cutter. Place cookies 1/2" apart on ungreased cookie sheets. Bake in preheated 325° oven for 15 minutes or until edges are barely golden. Cool on wire rack, handling carefully. Sprinkle the 1 tablespoon 10X sugar over hearts with cutouts. Spread rounded 1/4 teaspoon jam over center of each solid heart. Place cutout heart over solid heart. Store in airtight containers.

VALENTINE SUGAR COOKIES
Donnie Edmunds Rector - Kingsport, TN

1 C. powdered sugar
1 C. white sugar
1 C. (2 sticks) butter
   (do not use whipped)
1 C. oil
2 beaten eggs

5 C. plain flour
1 tsp. soda
1 tsp. cream of tartar
2 tsp. vanilla
1/4 tsp. salt

Mix together; roll into balls; press with sugar coated glass or roll 1/4" thick and cut with heart-shaped cookie cutter that has been dipped in flour. Bake at 325° about 10 to 12 minutes, on ungreased cookie sheet. Place dough in refrigerator while cookies are baking.
Note: Dough handles better if chilled for 1/2 hour before ready to use.

CRAN/APPLE SHERBET

1/4 C. very cold water
1/2 C. canned whole-berry
   cranberry sauce

1 14-oz. can pineapple chunks,
   drained and pieces frozen

Whirl in blender or food processor just enough to reach sherbet consistency. Serve immediately or freeze. Garnish with whole cranberries or sprigs of mint. Makes 4 servings.
Lovely in sherbet or parfait glasses.

To frost grapes, wash bunches of grapes in cold water. Drain. Dip each bunch in slightly beaten egg whites. Roll in granulated sugar. Let rest on wax paper. Beautiful garnish for hams, pork tenderloin or eye of round roasts.

. . . hearts go home for the holidays

LEMON CHEESE FILLING/SAUCE

12 egg yolks, beat until frothy
    with a wire whisk
1 C. lemon juice from concentrate

4 C. granulated sugar
1 C. butter or margarine

Place ingredients in top of double boiler over very hot water (not boiling). Cook for 50 to 60 minutes. Stir every 5 minutes. Store in refrigerator.

Use as filling for tarts or meringues or serve as sauce over pound cake slices. This is a very old recipe.

PINK PARFAIT

1 can cherry or strawberry pie filling
1 can sweetened condensed milk
1 (15 1/2-oz.) can crushed pineapple
1/4 C. lemon juice

1 C. pecans, coarsely chopped
Maraschino cherries or
    fresh strawberries, for garnish

Combine all ingredients and chill thoroughly. Serve in chilled parfait glasses on a small glass plate. Top with a fresh strawberry or cherry.

PUFF PASTRY HEARTS

1 sheet frozen puff pastry, thawed
2 T. sugar

1/2 tsp. ground nutmeg or
1/2 tsp. ground cinnamon

Roll pastry on very lightly floured surface into a 10x12" rectangle. Using a heart-shaped cookie cutter (approximately 3"), cut out hearts. Place on baking sheet. In a small second bowl, combine sugar and choice of spices. Sprinkle on "hearts". Bake at 350° for 12 to 15 minutes until puffed and lightly browned. Cool on a wire rack. Store airtight.

Note: These hearts may be placed over fresh strawberries or other fresh berries sweetened with sugar.

VALENTINE TARTS

16 oz. cream cheese, softened
2 eggs, beaten
3/4 C. granulated sugar
1 tsp. vanilla extract

10 vanilla wafers
10 maraschino cherries
10 cupcake paper liners

In a mixing bowl, cream cheese with sugar. Add eggs and vanilla. Place paper liners in muffin tins. Put a vanilla wafer in each liner (rounded side up). Pour cream cheese mixture over each layer. Bake at 350° for 20 minutes. Garnish each with a cherry on top. Refrigerate until ready to serve. Makes 10 servings.

. . . hearts go home for the holidays

St. Patrick's Day

- PARTY FOODS -

SHAMROCK TEA SANDWICHES (CUCUMBER)

1 sm. onion, peeled and quartered
1 lg. cucumber, cut in chunks
1 8-oz. pkg. cream cheese, softened
1/4 tsp. salt

Dash garlic powder
Dash cayenne pepper
3 drops green food coloring

In a food processor or blender, chop onion and cucumber 3 to 5 seconds. Scrape sides of processing bowl or blender with rubber spatula. Process or blend again for 3 to 5 more seconds. Remove vegetables and drain well. Add remaining ingredients to drained cucumber-onion mixture. Stir to blend. Chill slightly. Spread on thin sliced wheat and white bread, cut into shamrock shapes with a cookie cutter.

Note: This is enough to spread two 16-ounce loaves of bread. Very pretty served on a dark green glass plate, lined with a lace paper doily.

BELFAST BROCCOLI DIP

1 med. onion, chopped
1 4-oz. can mushroom stems and
  pieces, drained
1 T. butter
1 roll Kraft garlic cheese

1 (10 3/4-oz.) can mushroom soup
1 10-oz. bx. frozen chopped broccoli,
  cooked and drained
Dash Worcestershire sauce
Salt, to taste

Saute onion and mushrooms in butter in a saucepan. In a double boiler, melt cheese. To cheese, add mushroom soup and all remaining ingredients. Serve warm in chafing dish with crackers.

HOT CORNED BEEF DIP

1 8-oz. pkg. cream cheese, softened
2 T. milk
3/4 C. chopped corned beef
2 T. minced onion

2 T. minced green pepper (optional)
1/8 tsp. pepper (freshly ground
  is best)
1/2 C. sour cream

Combine all ingredients. Pour into baking dish (one from which dip will be served). Bake at 350° for 20 minutes until center is firm. Makes 2 cups.

Good as a hot dog dip on crackers or as spread on rye or pumpernickel party bread.

The old person is a child twice.

However long the road there comes turning.

The three things that run swiftest are a stream of fire, a stream of water, and a stream of falsehood.

PISTACHIO CHEESE BALLS

1 C. pistachios (red shell)
2 T. horseradish
1 sliced dill pickle
2 tsp. capers

1 green onion with top, cut in 1" pieces
1/2 tsp. salt
8 oz. cream cheese, softened
1/2 C. toasted slivered almonds

Chop pistachios in blender; set aside. In blender, mix horseradish, dill pickle, capers, green onion, salt and cream cheese. Blend until smooth and add almonds. Blend a second or two, leaving the nuts in little pieces. Shape mixture into balls, roll in chopped pistachios, coating thickly, and chill until serving time. Serve on picks. Makes 36.

- BEVERAGES -

IRISH COFFEE

1 1/2 tsp. sugar
1 jigger Irish whiskey (1 1/2 oz.)

Hot strong black coffee
Chilled whipped cream

In heated, stemmed Irish whiskey glass, stir sugar and whiskey. Pour in coffee to within 1" of top of glass. Top with whipped cream. Makes 1 serving.

EMERALD ISLE PUNCH

1 46-oz. can unsweetened
   pineapple juice
1 12-oz. can frozen orange juice
3 lb. sugar
1 gal. hot water

1 gal. cold water
6 pkg. lime Kool-Aid
4 qt. ginger ale (Canada Dry)
1 lime, sliced thin

Bring hot water to a boil and add sugar. When sugar has melted, take off burner and add Kool-Aid. Stir until dissolved. Add 1/2 of cold water; add orange juice and pineapple juice. Divide equally into 3 gallon jugs -- use about 1 1/3 bottle of ginger ale to each gallon, when poured into punch bowl. Garnish with lime slices.

IRISH WHISKEY PUNCH

1 jigger Irish whiskey
1 1/2 tsp. brown sugar
Cloves, to taste

Sliced lemon
Boiling water

Warm a glass goblet and put in the brown sugar with enough boiling water to dissolve it. Add the whiskey, cloves and sliced lemon. Add more boiling water to fill the goblet.
Traditional Irish punch.

ST. PAT'S PUNCH

8 pkg. lime powdered drink mix
6 C. sugar
3 6-oz. cans frozen lemonade

2 46-oz. cans pineapple juice, chilled
3 gal. very cold water
1/2 gal. lime sherbet*

*Ice may used instead of lime sherbet.
Combine first 5 ingredients. Pour over lime sherbet in punch bowl or individual glasses. Makes 50 servings.

- SOUPS -

CABBAGE SOUP

1 lb. lean ground beef
1/2 tsp. garlic salt
1/4 tsp. garlic powder
1/4 tsp. pepper
2 stalks celery, chopped
1 16-oz. can kidney beans, undrained

1/2 med. head cabbage, chopped
1 28-oz. can tomatoes, chopped
   (liquid reserved)
1 tomato can water
4 beef bouillon cubes
Chopped fresh parsley

In a Dutch oven, brown beef. Add all remaining ingredients except parsley; bring to a boil. Reduce heat and simmer covered for 1 hour. Garnish with parsley.

CREAMY POTATO SOUP

1/4 C. butter
2 med. onions, chopped
2 lb. red potatoes, peeled and sliced

3 C. milk
3 C. chicken stock

Melt butter in Dutch oven and add onions; cook slowly until tender but not brown. Add potatoes, milk and stock. Cover and cook over low heat until potatoes are tender, about 1 hour. Cool slightly and put soup through sieve or in food processor and puree. Reheat to serving temperature. Season with salt and pepper.

IRISH POTATO SOUP

6 slices thick bacon
2 lb. potatoes
2 oz. butter
1 1/2 pt. milk
1 1/2 pt. stock

1 C. cream
2 onions
Salt and pepper
Chopped parsley

Peel and slice the onions and simmer in the butter in a large pot. Peel and slice potatoes and add to the onions. Pour in the milk and stock; add salt and pepper. Cover and simmer for 1 hour. Add the cream. Fry the bacon until crispy. Use the bacon and parsley as a garnish.

- SALADS -

BLARNEY STONE SALAD

1 pkg. lime flavored gelatin
1 C. hot water
A few drops green food coloring
1 T. vinegar
3 carrots, shredded

1/2 C. salted peanuts, finely chopped
1 20-oz. can crushed pineapple
   (do not drain)
Peanuts, for garnish
Mayonnaise

Dissolve gelatin in very hot water. Add a few drops of green food coloring. Stir well. Add vinegar, carrots, nuts and pineapple with juice. Mix well. Pour into a 9x9" glass dish and chill until firm. Cut in squares and serve on leaves of lettuce. Top with mayonnaise and garnish with a few peanuts.

HOLIDAY CABBAGE SALAD

2 med. heads fresh cabbage
Salt
Pepper
Garlic powder

Parsley or Morton's
   Seasoning & Parsley
1 pkg. Ranch buttermilk dressing*
Whole caraway or celery seeds
Paprika

*Can be made with yogurt and milk instead of the buttermilk.
Chop cabbage coarsely and cook (parboil) in small amount of water until a bright, fresh green color. Drain well and cool completely. Toss with dressing and top with a sprinkle of paprika. Chill well. Keep refrigerated.
Good with poultry, beef or pork.

FRUIT SALAD

3 kiwi fruits, peeled and
   sliced crossways
1 pt. strawberries, hulled and sliced

1 T. lemon juice
Sauce for Fresh Fruit

Peel kiwi and slice. Hull strawberries and slice (reserve a few whole ones for garnish). Pour lemon juice over and chill. When ready to serve, toss with Sauce for Fresh Fruit. Makes 4 servings.

Sauce for Fresh Fruit
1 C. oil
1/2 C. sugar
1/4 C. vinegar
1 tsp. salt

1 tsp. dry mustard
1 tsp. celery seed
1 tsp. paprika
1/2 tsp. grated onion

Mix dry ingredients; add oil and vinegar alternately, using a wire whisk to beat well. While adding wet ingredients, add onion. Keep refrigerated until serving.
Tasty topping for any combination of fresh fruits.

IRISH FLAG SALAD

1st Layer:
2 3-oz. pkg. lime Jell-O
2 C. hot water (boiling point)

2 C. cold water

Dissolve lime Jell-O in 2 cups hot water. Stir in cold water. Pour into 14x10x2" pan or dish. Chill until partially set.

2nd Layer:
1 3-oz. pkg. lemon Jell-O
1 C. hot water (boiling point)
1/2 C. miniature marshmallows
1 C. pineapple juice

1 8-oz. pkg. cream cheese, softened
1 sm. can crushed pineapple, drained
1 C. whipped cream
1 C. mayonnaise

Dissolve lemon Jell-O in 1 cup hot water in top of double boiler. Add marshmallows and melt. Remove from heat and add 1 cup pineapple juice and softened cream cheese. Beat together with spoon. Stir in drained pineapple. Cool slightly. Fold in whipped cream and mayonnaise. Chill mixture. Pour over partially set lime layer. Chill.

3rd Layer:
2 3-oz. pkg. orange Jell-O
2 C. hot water (boiling point)

2 C. cold water

Garnish:
Whipped cream

Green pistachio nuts (in red shells)

Dissolve orange Jell-O in 2 cups hot water. Add cold water. Chill. Pour over congealed lemon/cream cheese mixture layer. Chill until top layer is congealed. Slice into squares and serve on lettuce leaves. Garnish with whipped cream and shelled, red shell pistachio nuts. Makes 24 servings.

Takes a little time to do, but is a real "conversation piece" when served. Can be made the day before serving.

Variation: For Christmas salad, substitute cherry Jell-O for orange Jell-O. Salad will be red, green and white. Just change the color and flavor or Jell-O for other holidays as well.

IRISH SALAD

1 C. cold cooked chicken (white meat)
1/2 C. finely diced celery
1/2 C. finely diced cucumbers
1/2 C. mayonnaise
1 T. chopped chives

4 lettuce leaves
4 T. Green Goddess dressing
1 or 2 drops green food coloring
4 artificial or real shamrocks

Combine first 5 ingredients. Mix well. Chill. Serve on lettuce leaves. Top with Green Goddess dressing. Place a shamrock on top.

Handsome is as handsome does.

SHAMROCK SALAD

2 lg. green bell peppers
8 oz. cream cheese, softened
4 oz. cottage cheese
1 T. chopped pimiento

1/2 C. chopped nuts
1 #2 can pineapple rings
Green cabbage leaves

Cut the stem end off of peppers; remove seeds. Combine creamed cheese, cottage cheese, pimiento and nuts. Stuff peppers with mixture. Wrap in plastic wrap. Chill. Slice in 1/3" rings. Place pineapple rings on cabbage leaves and place "shamrock" pepper ring atop pineapple.

- BREADS -

BARMBRACK (IRISH FRUITCAKE)

7 C. all-purpose flour, sifted
2 tsp. ground allspice
1 1/2 tsp. salt
1 C. sugar
2 pkg. active dry yeast
1 1/2 C. warm water

1 1/2 C. milk
6 T. butter
2 1/2 C. seedless raisins
3/4 C. golden raisins
3/4 C. chopped fruit peel
        (half lemon, half orange)

Cream yeast with 1 teaspoon of sugar. Put milk and butter on low heat. Stir until butter melts. Pour into yeast mixture. Let stand in a warm place 10 to 15 minutes until frothy. Sift flour, salt, rest of sugar, nutmeg and cinnamon into a large bowl. Make a well in the center and pour in mixture and beaten eggs. Mix well. Turn onto a floured board; add fruit and peel. Knead until smooth and elastic. Place dough in greased 9x5" loaf pan. Put in warm place until dough reaches edge of pan (about 30 minutes). Bake in 350° oven for 40 to 50 minutes. Cool on wire rack.

Glaze:
Stir 1 tablespoon sugar and 2 teaspoons water over low heat until sugar is dissolved.

BELFAST BROWN BREAD

1 lb. coarse wheat meal
1/2 lb. flour
3/4 pt. sour milk*

2 tsp. salt
2 tsp. baking soda

*May use buttermilk or fresh milk.
Mix wheat meal with the flour; add soda and salt. Make a well in the middle and pour the milk in. Mix well. Then knead the dough into a ball. Flatten or roll out into a circle to 1/2" thick. Mark an "X" on the dough. Bake at 425° for 25 minutes. Then reduce heat to 350° and bake for 15 minutes longer. Let cool for 6 hours before cutting.

. . . hearts go home for the holidays

IRISH TEA BREAD

8 oz. brown sugar
16 oz. currants or raisins
3/4 pt. cold tea (not iced tea)

24 oz. self-rising flour
2 eggs

Soak first 3 ingredients overnight. Next morning, add flour and eggs. Bake in loaf pan for 1½ hours at 300°.

LUCK 'O THE IRISH BREAD

2 C. plain flour
4 tsp. baking powder
1/2 tsp. salt
1 T. sugar

3 T. Crisco shortening
2/3 C. milk
1/2 C. raisins
1 T. caraway seeds

In a large mixing bowl, combine flour, baking powder, salt and sugar. Cut in shortening with a pastry blender. Add all the milk at once and stir well. Add raisins and caraway seeds, folding them in gently and evenly. Pour out onto a lightly floured surface and knead 18 to 20 times. Place in a greased 9" round cake pan. Bake in a preheated 375° oven for 25 to 30 minutes. Slice into wedges and serve with butter and honey.

- SIDE DISHES -

IRISH NOODLES (GREEN)

1 1-lb. pkg. green noodles
1 tsp. minced garlic
1 C. butter or margarine, softened
1 tsp. salt
1 tsp. pepper

3 T. chopped fresh basil or
    2 tsp. dried basil
    (fresh is much better)
1 C. grated Parmesan cheese
Sprigs of fresh basil, for garnish

In a large pot, cook noodles according to package directions. Drain; put back in pot. Add remaining ingredients. Stir gently to coat noodles. Place on serving platter and garnish with fresh basil sprigs.
Very good and very easy!

ERIN POTATOES

6 med. potatoes, peeled and
   sliced in 1/2" rounds
1 green bell pepper, cut in rings
1 T. butter

1 tsp. salt
1/2 tsp. white pepper or a wee bit
   of cayenne pepper
Fresh shamrock or green pepper ring

Peel potatoes; slice. Slice pepper rings; remove seeds and veins. Boil in water to cover with salt, butter and pepper until tender. Serve hot. Makes 6 servings.

Garnish with a shamrock or uncooked green pepper ring in shape of shamrock.

Note: Potatoes may be mashed instead of sliced and boiled. Then chopped, boiled green peppers added.

HAGGERTY

3 med. potatoes
1 lg. onion
2 T. bacon fat

3/4 C. grated Cheddar cheese
Salt and pepper, to taste

Wash and pare potatoes, cut in paper-thin slices, and pat dry in a towel. Slice onion very thin. Heat half of bacon fat in a heavy frying pan and fill pan with alternate layers of potatoes and onion and cheese, finishing with potatoes. Sprinkle each layer with salt and pepper. Dot the top layer of potatoes with remainder of bacon fat. Cook over moderate heat until potatoes are almost tender. Turn the Haggerty carefully onto a platter, slip it top side down, back into the pan, and continue cooking until done. To serve, cut into wedges. Makes 4 servings.

IRISH POTATO SPINACH BAKE

6 to 8 lg. potatoes, peeled,
   cooked and mashed
1 C. (8-oz.) sour cream
2 tsp. salt
1/4 tsp. pepper

2 T. chopped chives or
   green onion tops
1/4 C. butter or margarine
1 10-oz. pkg. frozen chopped spinach,
   thawed and well drained
1 C. (4-oz.) shredded Cheddar cheese

In a large bowl, combine all ingredients except cheese. Spoon into a greased 2-quart casserole dish. Bake, uncovered, at 400° for 15 minutes. Top with cheese and bake 5 minutes longer. Yield: 6 to 8 servings.

. . . hearts go home for the holidays

GREEN RICE

2 eggs
2 C. milk
1/2 tsp. salt
1 onion, minced
1/2 C. melted butter or margarine

2 C. cooked rice
1 10-oz. pkg. frozen chopped broccoli,
   thawed and drained
2 C. grated cheese

Beat eggs, milk and salt together in a large mixing bowl; set aside. In a saucepan, saute onions in butter; stir in rice, broccoli, egg mixture and cheese. Pour into a buttered 9x13" glass baking dish. Bake at 350° for 45 minutes. Serves 12.

This dish may be made ahead and frozen before baking.

IRISH VEGETABLES

6 potatoes
1 C. milk
1/2 C. butter
1 head cabbage, shredded

2 ribs celery, chopped
2 leeks or sm. onions
Salt and pepper, to taste

Boil potatoes in salted water. Rice or mash potatoes and add milk and butter. Cook cabbage, celery and leeks until tender. Drain well. Add vegetables to potatoes, mixing lightly. If necessary, reheat. Season to taste. Serve with melted butter on top.

In every land hardness is in the north of it, softness in the south, industry in the east, and fire and inspiration in the west.

A wise woman is better than a foolish doctor.

Bare is the compassionless shoulder.

What is gathered meanly, it goes badly.

- MAIN DISHES -

IRISH SHISH KABOBS

3 lb. lamb, cut in 1 1/2" cubes
2 lg. lemons, juice and rinds
2 cloves garlic, minced
1 T. salt
1/2 tsp. freshly ground black pepper
1 tsp. rosemary leaves, crumbled

Pinch of sage
1/2 C. oil
1 1/2 T. red wine
Sm. parboiled onions
Green and/or red peppers
Mushroom caps

In a large glass or enamel bowl, place lemon juice and the rinds (cut in strips, not grated), garlic, wine and spices. Add the lamb and mix so the lamb is well-coated with the marinade. Cover with Saran and foil and refrigerate 5 hours or overnight. Be sure to turn at least 4 or 5 times. Thread meat on skewers, alternating the lamb and onions, green peppers and mushroom caps. Broil over hot coals until done to your liking, turning and basting with the marinade. Serves 6 to 8.

Serve with wild rice.

Note: Beef sirloin tips, pork tenderloin, large shrimp or chicken cubes may be substituted for lamb for other holidays.

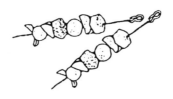

IRISH STEW

3 lb. mutton or lamb chops
6 carrots
5 onions
1 parsnip (optional)
1 turnip (optional)

2 1/2 C. water
8 to 10 potatoes
Thyme, salt, pepper and parsley,
   to taste

Cut the chops into large chunks and trim off the fat. Peel the potatoes and cut into chunks. Cut up the rest of the vegetables into chunks. In a large casserole dish or roasting pan, layer all the meat, then the potatoes, the carrots, onions and then the parsnip and turnip if desired. Season. Pour the water over all and cover tightly. Bake at 325° for 2 to 2½ hours.

. . . hearts go home for the holidays

CORNED BEEF AND CABBAGE

2 T. olive oil
1 med. cabbage, shredded or
  cut in 1" pieces
1 can corned beef, broken in 1" pieces

1 tsp. salt
1/2 tsp. pepper
1/4 C. vinegar

Place olive oil in saucepan or electric frying pan. Add the cabbage, corned beef, salt, pepper and vinegar. Cover tightly and cook, stirring frequently to prevent sticking for 10 to 15 minutes over medium heat. Makes 4 servings.
Very fast, very good!

TRADITIONAL CORNED BEEF AND CABBAGE

3 to 3 1/2 lb. corned beef brisket
1 lg. cabbage, cut in 8 to 10 wedges

5 whole peppercorns
1 T. sugar

In a large pot, cook brisket according to package directions. Add peppercorns. Add cabbage and sugar last 20 to 30 minutes of cooking time. Remove fat and slice corned beef into thin slices. Serves 8 to 10.
Note: An electric knife slices the corned beef perfectly.

CORNED BEEF & RYE CASSEROLE

1 14-oz. can sauerkraut
1 12-oz. can corned beef,
  broken into pieces
2 C. shredded Swiss cheese
1/2 C. mayonnaise

1/4 C. Thousand Island dressing
2 tomatoes, sliced
1/4 C. melted butter
1 C. rye bread crumbs

Layer, in order listed, all ingredients in a 9x13" glass baking dish. Bake at 350° for 20 to 25 minutes. Yield: 8 servings.

STUFFED GREEN PEPPERS

5 to 6 med. green peppers
3/4 C. uncooked brown rice
1 lb. lean ground beef
1 med. onion, chopped
1 8-oz. can tomato sauce
1/4 tsp. dried basil

1/4 tsp. dried oregano
1/4 tsp. dried thyme
1/2 tsp. salt
Pepper, to taste
1/2 tsp. instant beef bouillon

Remove tops and seeds from peppers. In a large kettle, bring water to boil; cook peppers for 5 minutes. Remove and drain. Cook rice according to package directions. In a skillet, brown beef and onion. Drain. Add tomato sauce, herbs, salt and pepper; cook 5 minutes. Stir in rice. Stuff peppers with the rice mixture. Place upright in a shallow dish. Bake at 375° for 15 to 20 minutes. Makes 5 to 6 servings.

CABBAGE AND SAUSAGES

6 sausages
4 C. cabbage, finely shredded

1/2 tsp. pepper
Salt, if necessary

Fry the sausages crisp and brown. Remove sausages and pour off all but 3 table-spoons of the fat. Put cabbage in pan, cover and cook until tender; add seasonings. Arrange on a hot dish and garnish with the sausages. Serve with mashed potatoes.

- DESSERTS -

IRISH WHISKEY CAKE

2 jiggers Irish whiskey
1 jigger sherry
2 1/2 C. milk
6 squares sponge cake
2 C. whipped cream

Almonds
Jam
2 eggs
1/4 C. sugar

Slice the squares of cake; spread with jam; put back together. Put in an 8 or 9" square pan with the whiskey and sherry. Make a custard from the eggs, milk and sugar; bake until done. Place the cooled custard on top of the sponge cake. Dab with the whipping cream and decorate with the almonds.

IRISH ALMOND CAKES

4 oz. butter
4 oz. castor sugar
3 oz. flour
1 tsp. baking powder
Water icing

2 oz. ground almonds
2 eggs
1/2 tsp. almond flavoring
2 oz. chopped almonds

Line an 11x7" shallow pan. Cream butter and sugar. Add each egg and beat well. Sift flour, baking powder and ground almonds, and stir in lightly to creamed mixture, adding flavoring. Spread into lined pan and bake for 35 minutes at 400°. Decorate with icing and chopped nuts. Cut into squares.

Don't spread your cloak any farther than you can cover it.

It is not the same to go to the king's house as to come from it.

Its own child is bright to the carrion crow.

. . . hearts go home for the holidays

APPLE PUDDENY-PIE

4 med. cooking apples
1 tsp. ground cinnamon
1/2 tsp. grated nutmeg
1/2 C. sugar
1/2 tsp. salt
1/3 C. water

2 tsp. fresh lemon juice
1 tsp. grated lemon rind
1/2 tsp. baking soda
1 C. quick-cooking oats
1/3 C. butter

Pare and core apples. Cut into eighths and place in greased baking dish about 10x16". Sprinkle with combined spices, sugar, and a little of the salt. Mix water, lemon juice, and grated rind and pour over apples. Add baking soda and remaining salt to oats; work butter into this mixture until crumbly. Spread oatmeal mixture over apples and bake in preheated moderate 375° oven for 40 minutes. Makes 4 to 6 servings.

GRASSHOPPER PIE

1 6-oz. pkg. real chocolate chips
1 (4 1/2-oz.) ctn. Cool Whip

5 T. creme de menthe
1 chocolate cracker crust

Melt chocolate chips in double boiler. Cool. Add Cool Whip and stir in creme de menthe. Pour into crust; refrigerate for 6 hours. Serve garnished with fresh sprig of mint and a chocolate leaf on each slice.

BLARNEY STONE COOKIES

2 C. rolled oats
1 C. packed brown sugar
1/2 C. sugar
1 C. all-purpose flour
1/4 tsp. salt

1 tsp. baking soda
1/4 C. hot water
1/2 C. shortening, melted and cooled
1 tsp. vanilla extract

In a mixing bowl, combine oats, sugars, flour and salt. Combine soda and water; stir into oats mixture along with shortening and vanilla. Roll into walnut-size balls. Place on greased cookie sheets. Bake at 350° for about 10 minutes or until golden brown. Remove from the oven; allow to stand 2 minutes before removing to a wire rack to cool. Yield: About 3 1/2 dozen.

CHOCOLATE CUPS
(For Strawberry or Cherry Ice Cream)

12 oz. white chocolate morsels or
  white candy coating
12 cupcake paper liners
Strawberry or cherry ice cream

Sm. whole fresh strawberries or
  maraschino cherries, for garnish
Ready to use cherry or
  strawberry glaze

In top of double boiler, melt chocolate or candy coating. Place paper liners in muffin tins. With a spatula, coat inside of paper liners. Refrigerate until ready to fill. To serve, remove papers and fill with 2 scoops of choice of ice cream. Serve on a lace paper doily-lined dessert plate. Garnish with cherries or strawberries and squiggle of glaze.

Variation: Use dark semi-sweet chocolate and fill with 2 scoops mini-chocolate chip ice cream.

IRISH CREME SAUCE

2 eggs, beaten
1 3/4 C. bourbon
1 14-oz. can sweetened
  condensed milk

1 pt. whipping cream
1 1/2 T. Hershey's chocolate syrup
3 T. water
1 1/2 tsp. vanilla

Beat eggs in blender. Add remaining ingredients; mix and refrigerate. Keeps 10 days. Serve over cakes or puddings.

The devil is good to his own in this world and bad to them in the next.

He who stares into the middle of the fire does be heavily in love.

What a person does not spend himself, his enemy spends it.

Pride goeth before a fall.

It is difficult to tame the proud.

While the cake is out the mouse will dance.

. . . hearts go home for the holidays

Easter

- PARTY FOODS -

MARZIPAN EASTER EGGS

4 oz. Marzipan (see Table of
    Contents - Easter: Desserts)

Food coloring mixed with water
Pastel colored sugar

Cut Marzipan into 12 equal parts. Roll between palms of hands shaping into "eggs". Paint with 1 drop food coloring mixed in 1/4 teaspoon water. Air dry for 20 to 25 minutes. Roll in colored sugars or granulated sugar.

EGG SALAD FILLING FOR SANDWICHES

6 hard-boiled eggs, peeled,
    mashed to fine consistency
2 T. mayonnaise
1 T. pickle relish

1 T. prepared mustard
Salt and pepper, to taste
1 tsp. grated onion (optional)

Combine all ingredients. Add more mayonnaise if needed so that mixture spreads easily. Serve hot or cold on slices of fresh white or wheat bread, plain or toasted, to make tasty sandwiches.
Note: Chopped stuffed green olives may be added.

LOW-CAL VEGETABLE DIP

2 C. (1-lb.) creamed cottage cheese
1 C. finely chopped, peeled and
    seeded cucumber
1 tomato, peeled, seeded and chopped

1/2 tsp. dried dillweed
1/2 tsp. salt
1/4 to 1/2 tsp. pepper sauce

Mix all ingredients in bowl. Cover and chill. Serve with fresh vegetables such as carrots and celery sticks, raw zucchini and cauliflower.

"A BUNCH OF CHEESE CARROTS" SPREAD

1/3 lb. sharp Cheddar cheese,
    finely grated
2 oz. cream cheese, softened

1/8 tsp. paprika
1/4 tsp. hickory salt
Parsley sprigs, for "carrot" tops

Grate Cheddar cheese; mix in cream cheese and seasonings. Pick the mixture up in your hands and roll it between your palms until smooth. Divide it into 5 equal pieces and roll each piece into the shape of a carrot about 5 or 6" long. (This is just like playing with play dough.) Put each cheese piece on a flat surface and roll with your open palm and fingers of your hand. Place the three "carrots" on the bottom and two on top. Put good size pieces of fresh parsley in the large end of carrots. Use the tip of a wooden spoon to make the little "dents" that real carrots have. This will look like a small bunch of carrots. Chill. Spread on crackers. Makes a lovely presentation.

ORANGE CREAM CHEESE SPREAD

1 8-oz. pkg. cream cheese, softened   **3 T. orange marmalade**

Combine cheese and marmalade. Shape in a ball or block and chill. Spread on gingersnaps, toast or banana bread. Yield: Approximately 1 cup.

- BEVERAGES -

PEACH COOLER

2 16-oz. cans sliced peaches in   **1 C. cultured low-fat buttermilk**
light syrup, drained and   **1/4 tsp. almond extract**
coarsely chopped   **2 1/2 C. vanilla ice milk**

Combine first 3 ingredients in container of electric blender; process until smooth. Add ice milk; blend 30 seconds or until smooth. Yield: 5 servings.

HURLEY'S HOLIDAY PUNCH
Nancy Hurley - Hartwell, GA

2 3-oz. pkg. lime Kool-Aid   **2 C. sugar**
1 46-oz. can pineapple juice   **2 qt. water**
1 qt. ginger ale   **Lime sherbet**

Mix together the dry Kool-Aid, pineapple juice, sugar and water. Chill in refrigerator. Just before serving, pour chilled mixture into punch bowl, add ginger ale, stir and float dollops of lime sherbet on top.

Vodka may be added if desired. Recipe may be doubled.

Note: This versatile punch base can be used for any holiday by changing the flavor and color of the Kool-Aid and sherbet. You may substitute the Kool-Aid and sherbet above with Tropical Punch Kool-Aid and pineapple sherbet or orange Kool-Aid and orange sherbet, etc., depending on the holidays.

Variation: For Halloween, make Witch's Brew by adding dry ice to little bowls of water and placing them around the punch bowl to give a spooky effect. Or, place plastic spiders, spider webs, bats, etc., in an ice ring made of 7-Up or ginger ale to give this brew a spooky effect. Omit sherbet if using the ice ring.

To prevent sliced or peeled apples, peaches, bananas and pears from turning brown, sprinkle orange, lemon, lime or pineapple juice on them.

- SOUPS -

CREAM OF CARROT SOUP

2 C. chopped carrots
1 sm. onion, sliced
1/4 C. butter
2 T. flour

Salt and pepper, to taste
2 C. scalded milk
1/2 C. hot evaporated skim milk
Chopped fresh parsley

Cook carrots; reserve cooking liquid. Set aside. Saute onion in butter until lightly browned. Add flour and stir to a paste. Scald milk in a saucepan. Add carrots to scalded milk. Pour mixture slowly over flour paste and onions, stirring constantly; add reserved cooking liquid and heat to boiling point. Add cream. Strain into heated soup tureen. Garnish with chopped parsley. Makes 6 to 8 servings.

VEGETABLES EN CONSOMME

4 C. consomme (chicken) or
    4 C. chicken broth
1 carrot, cut in shapes and cooked
1 sm. turnip, cut in shapes and cooked

1 sm. can LeSueur English peas,
    drained
1 sm. can asparagus tips, drained
Chopped chives
Heated croutons

Using a sharp knife or vegetable cutter, cut carrots and turnip slices into desired small shapes. Cook in salted water until tender (do not overcook). Use a small amount of consomme or broth to heat drained peas and asparagus tips. Add carrots and turnips. Pour into heated soup tureen. Bring remaining consomme or broth to a boil and pour over vegetables in tureen. Serve from tureen into soup bowls. Garnish with chopped chives. Serve with croutons. Makes 6 to 8 servings.

Note: Cut carrots and turnips into seasonal shapes. Potatoes may be substituted for turnips.

- SALADS -

COTTAGE CHEESE VEGETABLE SALAD

2 12-oz. ctn. low-fat cottage cheese
    (optional)
2 med. cucumbers, peeled and sliced

1 bunch radishes, sliced
1 bunch scallions, sliced
1 pt. sour cream

Combine all vegetables in a bowl. Add cottage cheese and season to taste. Top with sour cream. Serves 4 to 6.

If not using the cottage cheese, mix the sour cream into the vegetables. It's delicious either way.

PETER RABBIT SALAD

1 3-oz. pkg. cream cheese
1/3 C. grated carrot*
3 parsley sprigs

Spinach leaves
1 (8 3/4-oz.) can pineapple tidbits, drained

*Grate carrot onto paper towel; pat dry with another paper towel.

Divide cream cheese into 3 parts. With hands, shape each part to resemble a carrot 3" long. Roll "carrots" in grated carrot, coating completely. Insert a parsley sprig in top of each. Serve on spinach leaves; garnish with pineapple tidbits. Serve with mayonnaise, if desired. Makes 3 servings.

CREAMY FROZEN SALAD

2 C. dairy sour cream
2 T. lemon juice
3/4 C. sugar
1/8 tsp. salt

1 9-oz. can crushed pineapple, drained
1/4 C. sliced maraschino cherries
1/4 C. chopped pecans
1 banana, sliced

Blend cream, lemon juice, sugar and salt. Stir in remaining ingredients. Pour into 1-quart mold or cupcake papers. Freeze. Makes 8 servings.

DYED DEVILED EGGS

6 boiled eggs

Natural Dyes:
Beet juice
Turmeric
Blueberry juice
Cherry juice

OR:
1 drop desired food coloring
1 tsp. vinegar
1 tsp. water

Boil eggs. Remove shells. Slice in half lengthwise. Remove yolks; set aside. Cut a small slice off each egg half bottom so they stay put. Dye egg halves inside and out. Pat dry.

Deviled Egg Stuffing:
Egg yolks
2 T. Hellmann's mayonnaise
1 tsp. prepared mustard
Salt and pepper, to taste

1 T. pickle relish
Sm. sprig parsley or chopped chives or paprika, for garnish

Mash egg yolks with fork or use a ricer. Stir in mayonnaise, mustard, salt and pepper and relish to make thick paste. Stuffing may be piped into egg halves with pastry tube or by putting yolk mixture into heavy Ziploc bag with one bottom corner snipped off. Just twist the bag and fill each egg half. Garnish. Serve on lettuce leaves.

Note: Mixture may also be spooned into eggs.

EASTER BUNNY SALADS

8 canned pear halves
8 crisp lettuce leaves

32 orange sections
8 maraschino cherries

For each salad: Place pear half, cut side down, on lettuce leaf. Add 2 orange sections for each ear. Cut cherry into 6 slivers; use to make eyes, nose, mouth, and centers for ears. Serve with mayonnaise, if desired. Makes 8 servings.

Serve on paper doily-lined glass salad plates.

PEACHY PEACH SALAD

1 can peach halves, drained*
2 sm. jars baby food peaches*
1/2 C. blueberries, drained

3/4 C. toasted coconut
Lettuce leaves

*Apricots and baby food apricots may be substituted.

Toast coconut in a single layer on tray in toaster oven on light setting; set aside. Drain peaches; place on lettuce leaves in a glass plate (pitted side of peach up). Spoon the baby food into each peach half, top with blueberries and sprinkle with toasted coconut. Makes approximately 6 servings.

PINK DELIGHT EASTER SALAD

Sue Ashmore - Lincolnton, GA

1 lg. can crushed pineapple
1 lg. pkg. strawberry Jell-O
1 C. cottage cheese
1 sm. ctn. sour cream

1 lg. ctn. Cool whip
1/2 C. chopped pecans
1/2 C. coconut

Place pineapple in saucepan. Add Jell-O and cheese and beat until melted. Cool slightly. Mix sour cream and Cool Whip. Add to mixture. Fold in pecans and coconut. Chill 4 to 6 hours; overnight is best. Garnish with fresh strawberries.

MACARONI DINNER SALAD

1 C. cooked ham, cut in cubes
2 C. cooked elbow macaroni
4 hard-boiled eggs, sliced or diced
   (reserve a few slices for garnish)
1/2 C. finely chopped celery
1/4 C. chopped green pepper

1/4 C. minced onion
1/4 C. sweet pickle relish
1/2 C. Hellmann's mayonnaise mixed
   with 1 T. white vinegar
3 or 4 stuffed green olives,
   sliced, for garnish

Reserve a few slices of boiled egg for garnish. Slice olives and set aside. Mix remaining ingredients and chill. Serve in a large platter or in a large salad bowl garnished with egg and olive slices. Serves 4 to 6.

Note: This is pretty on a large platter surrounded by sprigs of parsley and cocktail tomatoes or sliced tomatoes.

TUNA SALAD MOLD

1 pkg. lemon Jell-O
1/2 C. cold water
2 T. lemon juice
1/2 C. mayonnaise
1/4 tsp. salt

1 can tuna fish
3/4 C. diced celery
2 T. diced pimiento
1/2 tsp. grated onion

Dissolve Jell-O in 1 cup hot water; add cold water and lemon juice, mayonnaise and salt. Blend with rotary beater. Pour in freezing tray and chill until firm, 1" from edge. Pour in bowl and beat until fluffy. Fold in other ingredients and pour in fish-shaped mold and chill until firm.

- BREADS -

EASTER BREAD

3 1/4 C. all-purpose flour
1/4 C. sugar
1 tsp. salt
1 pkg. active dry yeast
2/3 C. milk
2 T. butter or margarine, melted
2 eggs, at room temperature

1/4 C. diced candied orange peel
1/4 C. diced candied citron
1/4 C. chopped almonds
1/2 tsp. anisee
5 raw eggs in shells, plain or colored
Confectioner's sugar frosting
Tiny multi-colored candies

Measure flour onto piece of wax paper. Combine 1 cup flour and next 3 ingredients in large mixing bowl. Add milk to butter, then gradually add to dry ingredients. Beat at low speed of electric mixer, 2 minutes, scraping sides of bowl occasionally. Add first 2 eggs and 1/2 cup flour. Beat at medium speed, scraping sides of bowl occasionally, 2 minutes or until thick and elastic. With wooden spoon, gradually stir in just enough flour to make a soft dough that leaves sides of bowl. Turn out onto lightly floured board, shape into a ball and knead 5 to 10 minutes or until smooth and elastic. Put in greased bowl, turning to grease top. Cover and let rise in warm place free from drafts 1 hour or until doubled in bulk. Combine fruits, almonds and aniseed. Punch down dough, turn out on lightly floured board and knead in fruit mixture. Divide in half and roll each piece in a 24" rope. Twist ropes loosely together and shape in a ring on greased baking sheet. Arrange eggs in shells in empty spaces in twist. Cover and let rise in warm place 40 minutes or until doubled in bulk. Bake in preheated 350° oven for 30 to 35 minutes. Remove to rack; cover with towel. Cool, frost and sprinkle with candies.

A tall 3" candle in the center of the bread ring turns this into a lovely edible centerpiece.

Variation: Use as Christmas bread substituting candied fruit for eggs and centerpiece.

HOT CROSS BUNS

1 pkg. active dry yeast or
   1 cake compressed yeast
1/4 C. water*
1 C. milk, scalded
1 tsp. salt
1/2 C. sugar

1/2 C. shortening
4 1/2 C. sifted all-purpose flour
3 egg yolks, slightly beaten
1/2 tsp. ground cinnamon
1/2 C. currants
Melted butter

*Use very warm water (105 to 115°) for dry yeast; use lukewarm (80 to 90°) for compressed.

Sprinkle dry yeast or crumble cake into water. Let stand a few minutes, then stir until dissolved. Pour hot milk over salt, sugar, and shortening and cool to lukewarm. Add yeast and 2 cups flour, beat well, and let rise until light. Add egg yolks, then remaining flour mixed with cinnamon. Add currants. Knead; put in large greased bowl. Brush top of dough with melted butter. Cover, and let rise until doubled in bulk. Shape into small round buns and place close together in greased pan. Let rise until doubled in bulk. With a very sharp knife or single edge razor blade, cut a cross just through the top surface of each bun. Bake in preheated hot 400° oven for 15 minutes, brush with melted butter, and continue to bake for 5 minutes more. Cool on a rack. If desired, brush each cross on bun with a simple frosting made of confectioner's sugar moistened with water. Makes 1 1/2 to 2 dozen.

PARKER HOUSE ROLLS

1 C. milk
5 T. sugar
1 T. salt
1 cake yeast

1 C. lukewarm water
6 C. sifted flour
6 T. melted shortening

Scald milk; add sugar and salt; cool to lukewarm. Dissolve yeast in lukewarm water and add to lukewarm milk. Add 3 cups flour and beat until perfectly smooth. Add melted shortening and remaining flour or enough to make easily handled dough. Knead well. Place in greased bowl. Cover and set in warm place, free from draft. Let rise until doubled in bulk, about 1½ hours. Roll out 3/8" thick, and cut with 2 1/2" biscuit cutter. Crease heavily through center with dull edge of knife and brush very lightly with melted butter. Fold over in pocketbook shape. Place close together in well-greased shallow pans. Cover and let rise until light, about 1 hour. Bake in hot 425° oven about 20 minutes. Serve hot with butter.

When making cornbread, muffins or cornsticks, always heat oil or shortening in pan or tins in a preheated hot oven. Makes a nice brown crust.

POPPY SEED MUFFINS

2 C. all-purpose flour
1/4 C. poppy seeds
1/2 tsp. salt
1/4 tsp. baking soda
1/2 C. butter, room temperature

3/4 C. sugar
2 eggs
3/4 C. sour cream
1 1/2 tsp. vanilla

Preheat oven to 375°. Grease a 12-cup muffin tin (or use small muffin tins). Combine flour, poppy seeds, salt and baking soda in small bowl. Using electric mixer, cream butter with sugar until thick and light. Beat in eggs 1 at a time. Blend in sour cream and vanilla. Gradually beat in dry ingredients. Spoon batter into prepared tin. Bake muffins until tester inserted in centers comes out clean, about 20 minutes (for large muffins). Cool 5 minutes in tin on rack. Remove from tin and cool completely. Makes 12 large muffins.
Can use small muffin tins for 24 muffins.

ONE HOUR YEAST ROLLS

1 pkg. yeast
3/4 C. water
1 T. sugar

1/4 C. shortening
1/4 tsp. salt
2 C. flour*

Dissolve yeast in water. Mix in sugar, shortening, salt and flour. Make 12 rolls; put on greased pan and let rise for 1 hour. Bake at 450°.
*If plain flour, use 1 1/2 teaspoons baking powder. If self-rising flour, don't use baking powder.

- SIDE DISHES -

ASPARAGUS CASSEROLE

2 tall cans whole asparagus
5 hard-boiled eggs, sliced thinly
2 oz. pimiento, chopped
1/3 lb. Velveeta cheese

1/3 C. condensed milk
2 T. cornstarch
1/2 tsp. salt

Drain asparagus; slice boiled eggs; chop pimiento. Layer in order in casserole dish. Set aside. In a saucepan, combine Velveeta cheese, condensed milk, cornstarch and salt. Cook until cheese melts and mixture thickens slightly, stirring constantly. Pour evenly over asparagus mixture in casserole dish. Bake at 325° for 30 minutes.

ASPARAGUS-ENGLISH PEA CASSEROLE

Wanda M. Holloway - Lincolnton, GA

1 sm. can asparagus
1 can English peas
1 can cream of mushroom soup
1 C. cheese, grated

2 eggs, hard-cooked, chopped
3/4 C. Pepperidge Farm dressing (dry)
1/4 stick butter, melted

Drain peas and asparagus; mix with soup, cheese and eggs. Cover with 3/4 cup dressing and drizzle with melted butter. Bake for 30 minutes at 350°.

ASPARAGUS IN LEMON RINGS

1 lg. can fancy whole asparagus
spears, rinsed in ice water and
drained or 1 lb. fresh asparagus,
cooked until just tender

2 med. lemons, sliced into
1/3" thick rings, pulp removed

Divide asparagus into 6 equal bunches. Slip each bunch into lemon ring. Serve hot or cold.

BROCCOLI CASSEROLE

2 pkg. frozen, chopped broccoli
1 C. mayonnaise
1 C. sharp Cheddar cheese, shredded
2 eggs, beaten
2 C. Pepperidge Farm stuffing

1/2 C. butter or margarine, melted
1/2 tsp. salt
1/8 tsp. pepper
1 10-oz. can cream of mushroom soup
4 T. minced onion

Cook broccoli according to package directions; drain. Set aside cheese, butter and stuffing. Mix remaining ingredients and pour into buttered 9x13" casserole dish. Bake at 350° for 30 to 45 minutes. Add stuffing, mixed with melted butter and sprinkle cheese on top during last 5 minutes. Makes 8 servings.

QUICK CREAMY CABBAGE

4 C. shredded cabbage
1/2 C. water
2 T. flour

1 C. milk
1 tsp. salt
1/8 tsp. pepper

Cook cabbage in water 5 minutes. Sprinkle flour over cabbage; mix well. Add remaining ingredients. Cook and stir until thickened. Makes 4 servings.

CARROT CASSEROLE

12 lg. carrots, sliced and cooked in salted water until tender

1/2 lb. Velveeta cheese, cut in 1/2" slices
1/2 C. bread crumbs, for topping

Drain carrots; place half of them into a buttered 9x13" casserole dish. Cover with Velveeta cheese slices, then top Velveeta cheese with remaining carrots. Set aside. Pour Sauce over carrots. Do not stir. Top with bread crumbs. Bake uncovered at 350° for 30 minutes. Makes 8 servings.

Sauce:
1/2 C. butter
1/4 C. flour
1 sm. onion, chopped
1 tsp. salt

1/8 tsp. pepper
1/2 tsp. dry mustard
1/4 tsp. celery seed
2 C. milk

In a saucepan, melt butter and flour. Add remaining ingredients. Cook on medium heat until thick.

COCONUT CARROT RING

1 1/2 C. all-purpose flour
1 1/2 tsp. baking powder
1/2 tsp. salt
1 tsp. cinnamon
1 C. sugar
1 C. oil
2 eggs

1 C. finely grated carrots
1/2 C. chopped almonds
1/2 C. golden raisins
2 2/3 C. (7-oz.) flaked coconut
1 16-oz. can prepared cream cheese frosting

Mix flour, baking powder, salt and cinnamon. Beat sugar and oil at medium speed of electric mixer until well mixed. Stir in flour mixture. Add eggs, one at a time, beating well after each addition. Stir in carrots, nuts, raisins, and 2/3 cup of coconut. Pour into greased and floured 9" Bundt pan or 6-cup ring mold. Bake at 350° for 35 minutes or until cake tester inserted in center comes out clean. Cool in pan for 15 minutes. Remove from pan and finish cooling on rack. Frost with cream cheese frosting and cover thickly with remaining coconut.

GLAZED CARROTS

2 T. butter
1 lb. carrots, sliced thinly
1/4 tsp. grated orange peel

2 T. orange juice
Pinch of dried marjoram
1 T. maple syrup

Place all ingredients in a skillet. Cook 20 to 25 minutes over low heat until carrots are well glazed and tender. Stir to prevent sticking. Makes 4 servings.

CAULIFLOWER CASSEROLE

1 med. head cauliflower,
   broken into flowerets
1/2 C. Hellmann's mayonnaise
1/2 C. grated sharp Cheddar cheese

1/2 tsp. dry mustard
1/4 tsp. salt
1/8 tsp. cayenne pepper

Wash flowerets. Cook in salted water; drain. Place in casserole dish. Combine remaining ingredients and spread evenly over cauliflower. Bake uncovered at 400° for 10 to 12 minutes. Serves 4.

Note: Pepper Jack (Monterey) cheese may be substituted for Cheddar cheese.

EGGPLANT CASSEROLE

1 eggplant
1 C. chopped celery
1 green pepper, sliced
4 T. shortening

1 1-lb. can tomatoes
Salt and pepper
Bread crumbs
Grated cheese

Peel and dice eggplant. Boil eggplant and celery until tender. Drain. Saute green pepper in shortening. Add tomatoes and seasonings to taste. Alternate layers of eggplant and tomato mixture in a greased casserole dish. Sprinkle with crumbs and cheese. Bake at 350° for 20 minutes or until thoroughly heated.

EGGPLANT PARMESAN

1 med. eggplant, sliced 1/2" thick
1 egg, beaten with 2 T. water
1 C. seasoned bread crumbs
1 pkg. sliced mozzarella cheese

1 8-oz. can tomato sauce
Oil, for frying
Parmesan cheese

Preheat oven to 325°. Slice eggplant leaving skin on. Dip in beaten egg and then in bread crumbs. Refrigerate about 1 hour. Heat oil in large skillet and fry eggplant until brown on both sides. In a baking dish, spread 2 tablespoons of tomato sauce and then slices of eggplant. Top each piece with a slice of mozzarella cheese, then spread with remaining tomato sauce. Sprinkle with Parmesan cheese and bake at 325° for about 15 to 20 minutes until cheese melts.

Use whole green beans or asparagus spears tied in bunches with blanched green onion tops. Wrap a strip of the onion top around 10 or 12 beans and tie in a bow. Place on a platter or around roast or ham.

FRUIT COMPOTE

1 T. granulated sugar
1/2 tsp. freshly grated lime peel
2 tsp. fresh lime juice
1 sm. pineapple (about 2 1/2 lb.), peeled, cored and cut in small chunks

1 lg. kiwi fruit, peeled, halved lengthwise and cut crosswise in thin slices
1 pt. fresh strawberries, rinsed, drained, hulled and cut in half lengthwise (3 C.)
1 T. sesame seeds, toasted

Mix sugar, lime peel and juice in large bowl. Add pineapple and kiwi fruit; toss to coat. Let stand at room temperature 15 minutes or until sugar dissolves; stirring 2 or 3 times. Gently stir in strawberries. Just before serving, sprinkle with sesame seeds. Serve immediately or prepare 45 minutes to 1 hour before serving.

PEAS AU GRATIN

2 pkg. frozen English peas, cooked and drained
2 5-oz. cans sliced water chestnuts, drained

1 can cream of mushroom soup
1 1/2 C. grated sharp Cheddar cheese

Combine ingredients in order listed; mix well. Place in lightly greased 9x13" casserole dish. Bake at 350° for 25 to 30 minutes. Makes 6 to 8 servings.

BAKED PINEAPPLE

2 lg. cans pineapple chunks
1 C. granulated sugar
5 T. cornstarch

1 3/4 C. sharp Cheddar cheese, grated
1/2 C. margarine or butter, melted
2 C. Ritz cracker crumbs

In a saucepan, combine pineapple and juice with sugar and cornstarch. Cook over medium heat until sugar is melted. Pour into a buttered 9x13" casserole dish. Mix cheese, melted butter and cracker crumbs; spread on top. Bake uncovered at 350° for 35 to 40 minutes. Serves 10.

SUPER POTATOES
Wanda M. Holloway - Lincolnton, GA

9 med. potatoes
1/2 C. butter
2 C. Half and Half
1 tsp. salt

8 oz. Cheddar cheese, shredded
Dried minced onion, to taste
Pepper, to taste

Boil potatoes until tender. Cool, peel and slice 1/2" thick. Place in 9x13" casserole dish. Top with cheese. Heat together butter, Half and Half, and salt until butter melts. Pour over potatoes and cheese. Bake at 350° for 1 hour.

ORANGE RICE

1/4 C. chopped onion
1 C. chopped celery
1/4 C. butter or margarine
2 T. frozen orange juice concentrate

1 1/4 C. water
1/2 tsp. salt
1 1/3 C. rice

In a saucepan, saute onion and celery in butter or margarine; add orange juice, water and salt. Bring this to a boil. Add rice and cook as package directions say. Makes 4 to 6 servings.
Very tasty! Good with pork.

SOUTHERN SPINACH CASSEROLE

3 pkg. frozen spinach
2 3-oz. pkg. cream cheese
1 T. grated lemon rind
Salt and pepper, to taste

Dash of nutmeg
1 pkg. Pepperidge Farm dressing mix
1/2 stick margarine

Cook frozen spinach in small amount of water. Drain; while hot, add the cream cheese, lemon rind, salt, pepper and half of margarine and nutmeg. Mix slightly. Top with Pepperidge Farm dressing that has been crushed into crumbs and mixed with margarine. Bake for 25 minutes at 350°.
Note: May be made in individual molds as well.

BECHAMEL SAUCE

2 C. milk, heated
1/4 C. butter
1/2 sm. onion, minced

1/4 C. all-purpose flour
Salt and white pepper

Saute onion in butter until soft but not brown. Stir in flour. Gradually add milk. Stir until smooth. Salt and pepper to taste. Simmer for 15 minutes, stirring often. Strain through a sieve and serve over vegetables.

Scissors work well for removing tough stems from collards or turnip greens and cabbage.

For easy clean up, rinse saucepan with very cold water before heating milk.

- MAIN DISHES -

BETTY'S CHICKEN CASSEROLE
Betty Wilkins - Prosperity, SC

2 10-oz. pkg. frozen broccoli,
   cooked and drained
2 C. cooked, deboned chicken,
   cut in bite-size pieces
1 C. Hellmann's mayonnaise

1 can cream of chicken soup
1 can cream of mushroom soup
1/2 tsp. curry powder
1 tsp. lemon juice

Place cooked, drained broccoli in bottom of buttered 9x13" casserole dish. Top with cooked chicken. Mix remaining ingredients and pour over chicken. Top with following in order listed: 1/2 cup seasoned bread crumbs, 1/2 cup shredded cheese and 1 tablespoon melted butter. Bake at 350° for 30 minutes. Serve hot.

CHICKEN DIVAN

1 10-oz. pkg. frozen broccoli spears,
   cooked as per directions
4 chicken breasts, boiled and deboned
Salt, to taste
2 tsp. lemon juice
2 T. butter

3 T. grated Cheddar cheese
1/3 C. cooking sherry
1 can cream of chicken soup
1 C. bread crumbs
Butter, melted

Drain cooked broccoli spears. Arrange in buttered casserole dish. Cook chicken with salt to taste. Arrange chicken over broccoli. Combine lemon juice, cooking sherry and soup. Pour over chicken. Sprinkle bread crumbs over top and drizzle with butter. Sprinkle grated cheese over. Bake at 350° for 30 minutes.

CHICKEN PIE

1 3-lb. chicken, boiled in
   salted water and deboned
1 onion, chopped
2 carrots, sliced thinly

1 C. celery, sliced
2 C. chicken broth (reserved
   from cooking chicken)
1 can cream of chicken soup

In a large pot, cook chicken, onion, carrots and celery in water enough to cover. Salt to taste. Remove skin and bones; cut chicken in bite-size pieces. Place in a 9x13" baking dish. Mix chicken broth with soup in a saucepan and heat until boiling. Remove from heat. With a slotted spoon, remove vegetables from broth and place over chicken. Cover with Crust and bake at 425° for 30 minutes.

Crust:
1 C. self-rising flour
1 tsp. salt
1/2 tsp. black pepper

1/4 tsp. poultry seasoning
1 C. buttermilk
1 stick butter or margarine, melted

Combine ingredients and spoon over casserole.

HERBED BAKED CHICKEN

1 (3 to 3 1/2-lb.) chicken,
   cut in serving pieces
1/2 tsp. thyme
1/2 tsp. marjoram
3/4 to 1 C. flour
3/4 C. fat or salad oil

1/2 tsp. rosemary
1 T. minced parsley
1/2 tsp. salt
1/4 tsp. pepper
3/4 C. water

Sprinkle chicken with thyme and marjoram; let stand for 30 minutes to 1 hour. Roll in flour; fry in hot fat just long enough to brown on both sides. Remove from fat; place in baking pan. Sprinkle with rosemary, parsley, salt and pepper. Pour water into frying pan; stir well. Pour liquid over chicken. Bake at 375° for 40 to 45 minutes. Yield: 4 to 5 servings.

BAKED CANNED HAM

2 1/4 C. coarse fresh bread crumbs
1/3 C. packed brown sugar (light)
2 T. cold butter or margarine,
   cut in 8 pieces

1 T. cider vinegar
1 3-lb. fully-cooked canned ham
2 T. Dijon mustard
Whole cloves

Heat oven to 325°. Have a shallow baking pan ready. In a medium-size bowl, mix bread crumbs and brown sugar until blended. Add butter; rub in with fingers until mixture is crumbly. Sprinkle with vinegar; stir until blended. Place ham in ungreased baking pan. Brush top with mustard, then crumble bread mixture over mustard. Press lightly with hands so crumbs adhere. With the back of a large knife, press a diamond pattern in crumbs. Insert cloves where lines intersect. Bake for 1 hour.

BAKED HAM SLICE

1 3-lb. 2" thick slice of ham
1/2 C. brown sugar
1 sm. jar apple jelly

2 T. prepared mustard
1 T. currants or small raisins

Rub ham slice with brown sugar. Place in 9x13" casserole dish or baking pan. Mix mustard and apple jelly in a bowl until fairly smooth. Fold in currants. Pour over ham slice. Bake at 350° until lightly browned (about 45 minutes). Serves 4 to 6.

Note: For easier cleanup, line baking dish with foil.

Never add salt to meat until it has been partially cooked or lightly browned. Salt added before cooking toughens meat.

HAM & EGG PIE

White Sauce:
2 T. butter
2 T. plain flour
1/2 tsp. salt

Few grains cayenne pepper
1 1/2 C. milk

In a saucepan, melt butter; add flour. Stir until smooth. Add salt, pepper and milk. Cook until thickened. Remove from heat.

Filling:
1 C. leftover baked ham, diced
2 boiled eggs, sliced (use egg slicer)
1 level T. dried chopped chives

Prepared pie crusts (box with
2 refrigerated crusts)

Line pie plate with crust. Place ham, eggs and chives in bottom. Pour White Sauce over top. Place second pie crust on top. Rub edges with a little water and seal; flute edges if you like. Prick top with fork several times. Bake in a preheated oven until golden brown, approximately 15 to 20 minutes. Slice in wedges and serve hot.

Note: A small can of English peas (drained) may be added to filling as well.

GLAZE FOR HAM

1/3 C. brown sugar, packed
1 tsp. dry mustard

1/4 C. unsweetened pineapple juice
1/4 tsp. ground cloves

Mix well. Brush on ham after skin has been removed during last hour of baking.

- DESSERTS -

COCONUT LAYER CAKE

1 C. shortening
2 C. sugar
4 eggs, separated
1 tsp. vanilla flavoring

3 C. plain flour
1/4 tsp. salt
3 tsp. baking powder
1 C. milk

Cream shortening and sugar. Add egg yolks and vanilla. Beat well. Add sifted dry ingredients alternately with milk. Fold in stiffly beaten egg whites. Turn batter into 3 or 4 well-greased cake pans. Bake at 350° for 30 minutes.

Eggs may be used whole.

Frosting:
1 3/4 C. sugar
2 T. Karo syrup

5 egg whites, stiffly beaten
1 C. water

Cook sugar, syrup and water until it spins a long thread. Pour the syrup over stiffly beaten egg whites, mixing well. In a saucepan, add 1 cup sugar, 1/2 cup coconut and 2 cups of water. Bring to a boil. Spoon this over cake layers, then put Frosting on top and sprinkle with coconut.

. . . hearts go home for the holidays

COTTON TAILS

1 angel food cake, cut into
  1 1/2" cubes

Coconut

Roll pieces of angel food cake in Meringue Frosting, then in a bowl of shredded coconut to coat. Place on wax paper.

These do not store well. Serve the same day they're made.

Meringue Frosting:
1 C. sugar
1/2 C. water

2 eggs whites
1/2 tsp. vanilla extract

Beat egg whites until stiff. Set aside. In a saucepan, combine sugar and water and cook over low heat until syrup will "spin a thread" (pick some syrup up in a spoon and pour it back into pan until it makes a "thread"). Pour syrup into beaten egg whites and beat until smooth and spreadable. Add vanilla. Mix well.

CHOCOLATE MOCHA PIE

1 8-oz. Hershey's almond bar
9 oz. Cool Whip
1 T. instant coffee

1 T. water
1 graham cracker crust

Melt candy in double boiler; cool. Combine with Cool Whip, coffee and water. Pour into graham cracker crust and refrigerate for 6 hours. Garnish with chocolate curls.

COCONUT PIE (OLD FASHIONED)

1 stick butter
1 1/2 C. granulated sugar
3 eggs, beaten
1 T. vinegar

1 tsp. vanilla
1 C. coconut
1 unbaked 9" pie shell

Cream butter and sugar; add eggs. Stir until smooth. Add remaining ingredients. Stir well and pour into unbaked pie shell. Bake at 325° for 1 hour.

For individual pie crusts, turn a muffin tin upside-down and fit pie crust around as many as you need. Slide the tin into a hot oven and bake until lightly browned. Fill with pie filling or creamed chicken or turkey, etc.

LEMON CHIFFON PIE

1 lg. can evaporated milk
1 pkg. lemon Jell-O
Rind of 2 lemons, grated

Juice from 3 or 4 lemons
1 C. sugar
1 C. hot water

Dissolve Jell-O in hot water. Put Jell-O in refrigerator until it begins to jell, then take out and whip. Freeze a can of milk until icy, then whip. When it begins to whip, add juice, rind and sugar. Whip until stiff. Fold Jell-O mixture into whipped milk mixture. Put into graham cracker crust or if you want a special pie, use the Meringue Nut Crust and chill. Makes 2 pies.

Meringue Nut Crust:
2 egg whites
1/2 C. chopped pecans
1/2 C. sugar

1/8 tsp. cream of tartar
1/8 tsp. salt
1/2 tsp. vanilla

Beat egg whites until frothy. Add cream of tartar and salt. Beat until it stands in small peaks. Add sugar gradually. Beat until very stiff. Fold in vanilla and nuts. Turn into greased pie plate and shape. Bake at 275° for 1 hour (45 minutes, then turn oven off and leave 15 minutes). Cool and fill.

LEMON ICEBOX PIE (UNCOOKED)

1 14-oz. can Eagle Brand milk
Juice of 3 lemons
3 eggs, separated

3 T. sugar
Grated rind of 1 lemon
Graham cracker crust

Beat egg yolks well, then add milk, sugar, lemon juice and rind. Top with Meringue.

Meringue:
3 egg whites
1/4 C. sugar

Pinch of cornstarch
Tiny pinch of salt

Beat egg whites until foamy. Gradually add sugar, cornstarch and salt until stiff peaks form. Spread on pie filling, spreading to edge of crust. Bake at 325° for 20 minutes or until lightly browned. Makes 6 to 8 servings.
Cool and refrigerate for several hours before serving.

PASTEL PIE

1 9-oz. ctn. Cool Whip
1 14-oz. can sweetened
   condensed milk
2 T. lemon juice
1 8-oz. can crushed pineapple, drained

1 pkg. frozen diced strawberries,
   thawed and drained
1 9" graham cracker crust
1 pkg. ready to use strawberry glaze

Combine Cool Whip, milk, lemon juice, pineapple, and strawberries. Mix well and pour into graham cracker crust. Chill for 4 to 6 hours.
To serve, slice in wedges and garnish with "squiggle" of glaze on top.

PINEAPPLE PIE

1 (5 1/4-oz.) pkg. instant
   vanilla pudding
2 C. dairy sour cream

1 8-oz. can crushed pineapple
   (with juice)
1 9" graham cracker pie crust
Whipping cream, whipped until stiff

Combine pudding, sour cream and pineapple and juice. Mix well. Pour into graham cracker pie shell. Top with whipped cream. Refrigerate for several hours. Slice and serve. Makes 6 to 8 servings.

PISTACHIO-PINEAPPLE PIE

1/4 C. butter or margarine, melted
2 C. flaked coconut
1 1/2 C. milk
1 env. whipped topping mix

1 pkg. (4-serving size) pistachio
   instant pudding and pie filling
1 (8 1/4-oz.) can crushed pineapple

Combine butter and coconut; press in 9" pie pan. Bake at 300° for 20 minutes or until golden. Cool. Blend milk, whipped topping mix, and pudding mix in mixer bowl. Gradually increase beating speed and beat at high speed for 5 minutes or until thick. Fold in drained pineapple. Spoon into pie crust. Chill 3 hours. Garnish with toasted coconut.

SUNRISE PIE

1 C. sugar
1 stick butter or margarine
2 eggs, beaten
1 tsp. vanilla

1/2 C. shredded coconut
   (canned or frozen)
1/2 C. golden raisins
1/2 C. chopped pecans
1 9" pie shell (unbaked)*

*Could use 8 or 10 individual tart shells instead of 1 large pie crust.
Combine all ingredients in order listed. Mix well and pour into unbaked pie crust. Bake at 300° for 1 hour. Makes 6 servings.

MARZIPAN

1 C. blanched almonds
1 tsp. almond extract

2 C. sifted confectioner's sugar
2 egg whites, beaten slightly

Grind almonds to very fine consistency in food processor or blender. Mix ground almonds, almond extract and sugar. Add 1 teaspoon of egg whites at a time; beat well after each addition with metal spoon. Add egg whites until mixture is moistened. Knead until smooth and firm. Roll into desired shapes. Makes approximately 1 1/4 cups.
Note: This is a very versatile recipe and is referred to in several other recipes in this book. If you use your imagination, you can shape just about anything with this.

MUD HENS

1 stick margarine
1 C. granulated sugar
3 eggs (reserve 2 egg whites)
1 1/2 C. all-purpose flour

1 tsp. baking powder
1 tsp. vanilla extract
1/2 C. pecans, chopped
1 C. brown sugar

Cream margarine and granulated sugar. Add 1 whole egg plus 2 egg yolks. Mix well. Add flour, baking powder and vanilla. Spread on bottom of buttered and floured 9x13" pan. Sprinkle nuts on top. Beat 2 egg whites until stiff; fold in brown sugar and spread on top of nuts. Bake for 15 to 20 minutes at 350°. Serve warm, cut into squares.

COCONUT TASSIES (TARTS)

Pastry:
1 1/3 C. sifted all-purpose flour
1/3 C. sugar
1/4 tsp. salt

3/4 C. butter or margarine
1 egg, slightly beaten

Sift flour with sugar and salt into medium bowl. With pastry blender or 2 knives, cut in butter until mixture is like coarse cornmeal. Stir in egg with fork. Knead slightly until mixture holds together. Wrap in wax paper; refrigerate several hours or until firm. Preheat oven to 375°. For each tart, pinch off about 1 teaspoon dough. Press into 2x2½" tartlet pans, to make lining 1/8" thick. Fill each with Filling, about 1 teaspoon for each. Set tartlet pans on cookie sheet. Bake tarts (about 24 at a time) 12 minutes or until the Filling is golden brown. Invert pans on wire rack; cool slightly. With spatula, gently remove tarts from pan. Makes approximately 4 dozen.

Filling:
1 egg
1 (3 1/2-oz.) pkg. flaked coconut

2/3 C. sugar

With fork, beat egg in small bowl. Add coconut and sugar; mix well.
Note: Tarts may be wrapped, then frozen. Let thaw about 1 hour before serving.

COLORED COCONUT

1 C. flaked coconut

Few drops of desired food coloring
mixed with 1/4 tsp. cold water

Spread coconut on a wax paper-lined cookie sheet. Mix a few drops of desired food coloring with 1/4 teaspoon water. Sprinkle over coconut in a jar. Cover jar and shake until coconut is colored. Let air dry before using.
Example: Green coloring for cupcakes to use on top of icing as "grass" for nest of colored jelly beans.

EGG CUSTARD

1 qt. Half and Half
1 C. granulated sugar

5 eggs, beaten
3 T. vanilla

Heat Half and Half (do not boil). In a mixing bowl, beat sugar and eggs together. Add to heated Half and Half. Pour into 8 to 10 individual custard cups or in a single glass baking dish. Cook on low. Stir in vanilla.

FROZEN EASTER EGG

3 pt. vanilla ice cream, softened
1 C. mixed candied fruit
1/4 C. light rum
1 C. heavy cream

2 T. sugar
Few drops red, blue, and
   yellow food color

In large bowl, combine ice cream with candied fruit and rum, mixing well. Do not let ice cream melt. Pack ice cream mixture into a 1½-quart melon mold. Freeze until firm -- several hours or overnight. To unmold: Wipe outside of mold with hot, damp dishcloth; unmold ice cream onto chilled serving platter. Freeze 15 minutes. Whip cream with sugar just until stiff. Use half of whipped cream mixture to frost ice cream. Return ice cream to freeze. Divide remaining whipped cream into 3 parts. Tint one part pink, one blue, and one yellow. Keeping colors separate, pipe whipped cream through desired decorating tip of pastry bag, decorating ice cream like an Easter egg. Freeze until firm. Then, freezer-wrap, label, and freeze until ready to use. To serve, cut crosswise into slices. Makes 8 to 10 servings.

PINEAPPLE SAUCE

2 C. whipping cream
2 T. powdered sugar

1 20-oz. can crushed pineapple,
   drained well

Chill mixing bowl and beaters in freezer. Beat whipping cream and sugar until stiff in chilled bowl. Add pineapple. Stir gently. Refrigerate until ready to use. Stir before serving. Use as a sauce over pound cake slices.

Add 1 teaspoon cornstarch to each cup of sugar when making fudge to make it smooth and creamy.

Grate cheese, chop nuts, shred coconut and do other time-consuming things ahead of time during holidays. Store in Ziploc bags and freeze. They'll be ready to use when you need them.

. . . hearts go home for the holidays

4th of July

4th of July Deviled Eggs
Red white blue

6 boiled eggs
1 drop red food color
" blue "
1 tsp vinegar ⟩ for dye
" water
stuff the eggs deviled
Peel - dip in red & 2 in blue
& 2 white dye one run.
cut in half - take our yolk
& devil
makes 12 halves
put tiny flags in stuffing if
want

Ellen - I goofed - sorry
wrote this on here instead
of my white paper! Haste
makes waste!

- PARTY FOODS -

RED, WHITE AND BLUE DEVILED EGGS

6 boiled eggs
1 drop red food coloring
1 drop blue food coloring
1 tsp. vinegar

1 tsp. water
Deviled Egg Stuffing (see Table of
   Contents - Easter: Salads)

Peel boiled eggs. Dye 2 of the peeled whole eggs in red coloring and 2 in blue. Leave 2 white. Let stand for 1 minute after dying. Cut in half lengthwise. Remove yolks. Set aside. Make stuffing for deviled eggs. Stuff colored egg halves. Makes 12.

Fun to take to 4th of July picnics.

Note: Small paper flags on toothpicks may be stuck in top of each egg half.

SWEET-SOUR MEAT BALLS
Betty Miller Wilkins - Prosperity, SC

Meat Balls:
2 lb. ground beef
2 eggs
1/2 C. bread crumbs

1/2 C. water
Salt, pepper and garlic, to taste or
   use steak salt, to taste

Mix ingredients; form into approximately 48 balls. Bake or fry until done. Set aside.

Sauce:
1 bot. chili sauce
1/2 C. grape juice

Juice of 1 lemon

In a saucepan, combine ingredients in order listed. Heat, but do not boil. Drop meat balls into sauce. Serve hot in chafing dish or crock pot using toothpicks.

BARBECUED PEANUTS

4 C. salted peanuts

1/3 C. bottled barbecue sauce

Stir peanuts and barbecue sauce together in a small bowl. Spread in a shallow baking dish. Bake at 300° for 10 to 15 minutes or until dry, stirring occasionally. Cool in baking dish. Store in airtight container. Makes 4 cups.

STUFFED DILL PICKLES

1 3-oz. pkg. cream cheese
2 T. mayonnaise
1 T. Worcestershire sauce

1/2 C. finely chopped walnuts
Few grains cayenne pepper
3 lg. dill pickles, cored

With a long, thin paring knife, core the pickles. Set aside. Combine cheese, mayonnaise, Worcestershire sauce, nuts and pepper. Stuff cored pickles. Chill for 2 hours. Slice 1/3" rounds crossways and serve.

PROSCIUTTO MELON BALLS

Watermelon
Cantaloupe
Honeydew melon

Lemon juice/lime juice
Prosciutto ham

Use a melon baller, scoop balls from each piece of fruit (as many as you need). Sprinkle with lemon or lime juice. Wrap each ball with a thin strip of prosciutto ham. Secure with toothpick. Chill and serve in hollowed out melon shell or in hollowed out pineapple half.

BAKED SALAMI

1 sm. whole salami
Hot mustard

1 loaf party rye bread

Score salami. Using sharp knife to make criss-cross design on top and sides of salami slice thinly. Bake at 250° for 1 hour. Serve with hot mustard or party rye bread.

FIRECRACKER TOMATOES

6 to 8 med. tomatoes,
peeled and sliced
2 to 3 jalapeno peppers, thinly sliced

Hellmann's mayonnaise
Saltine crackers (Premium original)
Salt and pepper

Peel and slice tomatoes. Add thinly sliced peppers. Put in a covered dish and refrigerate several hours. When ready to serve, put a small bowl of mayonnaise and a basket of saltine crackers on table. Transfer tomatoes and peppers to platter (or serve from original container). Spread a liberal amount of mayonnaise on a cracker. Top with a tomato slice and a pepper slice. Top with salt and pepper to taste. Serves 6.

Hot as a firecracker!

Note: Increase number of tomatoes and peppers to serve a larger crowd.

DIP FOR VEGETABLES

1 pt. mayonnaise
1 pt. sour cream
1 T. dried parsley

1/2 tsp. paprika
1/2 tsp. onion salt
1 1/2 T. seasoned salt

Combine all ingredients in a bowl; stir until blended. Chill and serve with fresh vegetables.

Sieved boiled egg yolks make a nice "yellow" garnish on canapes.

. . . hearts go home for the holidays

FIESTA STRATA

1 can refried beans
1/2 lb. ground beef,
  browned and drained
1/2 pt. sour cream mixed with
  1 pkg. taco seasoning mix
1 sm. can sliced black olives, drained

2 T. grated onion
1 garlic clove, finely minced
1 C. shredded Cheddar cheese
2 chopped tomatoes
1 sm. can chopped chilies
Taco chips

Layer ingredients in a casserole dish in order given. Serve with taco chips for dipping.

Very nice in a glazed terra cotta serving dish.

DEVILED HAM SPREAD

8 oz. deviled ham
1/2 C. toasted almonds, ground or
  chopped fine
1/4 C. Hellmann's mayonnaise
1 tsp. chopped capers

1 tsp. Worcestershire sauce
1 tsp. dry mustard
2 tsp. liquid from jar of
  sweet pickles

In a bowl, combine all ingredients. Mix well. Refrigerate in a tightly-covered container.

May be made several days ahead. Good to spread on crackers or party bread slices.

VIDALIA ONION SPREAD

Linda Holloway Cooper - Lincolnton, GA

1 C. coarsely chopped Vidalia onions
1 C. Hellmann's mayonnaise

1 C. grated Cheddar cheese
Paprika

Combine onions, mayonnaise and cheese. Pour into 1-quart baking dish. Sprinkle with paprika. Bake at 350° for 25 minutes. Remove from oven, blot top with paper towels to remove excess oil. Serve hot with Triscuits.

- BEVERAGES -

PICNIC LEMONADE

1 C. plus 2 T. sugar
1 1/4 C. water
8 C. ice water
1 1/2 C. fresh squeezed lemon juice

1 T. grated lemon rind
(yellow part only)
Thin lemon slices, sprigs of mint or
maraschino cherries, for garnish

In a saucepan, dissolve sugar in 1 1/4 cup warm water. Bring to a boil, reduce heat and simmer for 5 minutes. Stir a few times while simmering. Remove from heat. Refrigerate until cool. Mix sugar mixture with remaining ingredients. Serve in tall glasses of ice. Garnish.

Note: For pink lemonade, add juice from bottle of red maraschino cherries. Use cherries for garnish.

PLANTERS PUNCH

1/2 gal. orange juice
4 C. pineapple juice
Juice of 4 lemons
1/2 C. sugar

1 1/2 C. Jamaican rum or, to taste
Orange slices, cut in half
Maraschino cherries
Sprigs of fresh mint

Combine ingredients. Stir and chill. Stir again before serving. Serve over ice. Garnish. Makes 24 to 30 servings.

Note: A nice southern tradition is to place a railroad spike sprayed silver or gold on the table in front of a "spiked" punch bowl to indicate that it is!

SUMMER PUNCH

1 6-oz. can frozen orange juice
1 6-oz. can frozen lemonade

1 12-oz. can or bot. apricot nectar
2 1/2 C. pineapple juice (1 #2 can)

Add amount of water required on frozen juice directions. Mix with other juices. Chill and serve over ice. Makes approximately 3 quarts.

Use clear glass plates, cups and glasses on seasonal place mats for a delightful change from china and tablecloths.

- SOUPS -

BRUNSWICK STEW FOR A CROWD

6 lb. beef, ground
3 lb. pork, ground
1 3-lb. hen, ground
2 lg. onions, minced
6 cans tomatoes
6 cans whole kernel corn
2 lg. bot. catsup

1 lg. bot. Worcestershire sauce
4 potatoes
1/2 C. sugar
Salt and pepper, to taste
Hot pepper, if desired
1/2 C. vinegar
1 tsp. Tabasco sauce

Cook meat with minced onions. Grind all meats. Cook potatoes and mash. Mix all ingredients; cook on medium-low heat for 2 hours. Stew freezes well. Yield: 12 pints.

COLD CRAB BISQUE

2 cans cream of celery soup
1 soup can milk
1 soup can water
2 (6 1/2-oz.) cans white crab meat,
    rinsed in cold water and drained

2/3 C. finely chopped celery
1/8 tsp. ground mace
A few grains cayenne
Sprigs of parsley, for garnish

Beat soup, milk, water, cayenne and mace together with whisk or electric hand held mixer. Stir crab meat and celery into soup mixture (taking care that any bits of shell, etc., from crab have been removed). Chill for 3 to 4 hours. Serve cold in chilled soup bowls. Garnish with sprigs of fresh parsley or chopped fresh parsley. Makes 6 servings.
Wonderful on a hot day.

- SALADS -

BARBECUED BEAN SALAD

1 #303 can kidney beans, drained
1 #303 can baby lima beans, drained
1 #303 can barbecue beans, drained
1/2 C. chopped celery

1/2 C. chopped onion
1/4 C. chopped green pepper
1/4 C. chopped pimiento

Combine all ingredients. Set aside.

Sauce:
1/2 C. vegetable oil
1/4 C. wine vinegar
1/2 C. granulated sugar

1 tsp. salt
1/4 tsp. pepper

In a saucepan, combine all ingredients and simmer for 5 minutes. Pour over vegetables. Mix well and chill overnight. Serves 8 to 10.

PICNIC COLESLAW

Slaw:
2 C. shredded red cabbage   3 C. shredded green cabbage

Shred cabbages and mix with chilled dressing. Refrigerate until ready to serve.

Dressing:
1/3 C. Hellmann's mayonnaise   Salt and pepper, to taste
1/3 C. dairy sour cream   2 tsp. grated onion (optional)
3 T. cider vinegar   Several dashes Tabasco sauce
2 tsp. sugar   (optional)
1 tsp. dry mustard

Combine ingredients in a small bowl. Mix well. Chill for 1 hour.

THREE DAY SLAW & DRESSING

Slaw:
1 med. head green cabbage, shredded   1 green pepper, chopped
1 med. onion, chopped   1 sm. jar pimiento, chopped

Combine ingredients and set aside. Pour Dressing over slaw and mix well. Pour into a container with a tight-fitting lid. Cover and refrigerate for 3 days. Do not remove cover. Then stir and serve.

This is good with any meat, poultry or fish.

Dressing:
1/2 C. honey   2 tsp. sugar
1/2 C. cooking oil   2 tsp. salt
1/2 C. white vinegar   1 tsp. celery seed

Combine ingredients in a saucepan and bring to a hard boil. Pour over slaw.

COPPER PENNIES (MARINATED CARROTS)

2 lb. carrots, sliced and cooked   1/2 tsp. salt
2 sm. onions, sliced paper thin   1 tsp. marjoram
1 sm. green pepper, sliced paper thin   1/8 tsp. pepper
1 can tomato soup (undiluted)   1/3 C. vegetable oil or olive oil
1 C. granulated sugar   3/4 C. white vinegar
1 tsp. Worcestershire sauce   1 tsp. prepared mustard

Cook thinly sliced carrots in boiling water until just tender. Drain carrots and combine with remaining ingredients. Stir well. Cover and refrigerate until ready to serve. Best when marinated at least 2 days. Serve cold as is or bake at 375° for 1 hour to serve hot.

Note: This is a wonderful dish with fried fish or chicken.

CHICKEN SALAD EN CANTALOUPE

3 ripe cantaloupes, chilled
3 C. cooked (white meat) chicken,
   cubed about 1/2"
2 C. diced celery
2 1/2 C. seedless white grapes
1 1/2 C. mayonnaise

6 T. milk
1 1/2 T. chutney
1 1/2 tsp. curry powder
1/4 tsp. salt
Fresh mint sprigs, for garnish

About 2 hours before serving, combine cubed chicken, grapes and celery. Set aside. In blender on low speed, blend mayonnaise, milk, chutney, curry powder and salt until smooth. Pour over chicken mixture. Toss lightly with two forks until mixed. Cover and chill. When ready to serve, cut cantaloupes in half; scoop out seeds, etc., and scallop edges with sharp knife or leave plain. Fill each half with chicken salad. Garnish with a sprig of mint. Serve on glass dessert plate. Makes 6 servings.

Note: This is both beautiful and delicious and can be made ahead of time.

MISS LORENA'S CHICKEN SALAD
Lorena Goolsby - Lincolnton, GA

1 whole chicken, cooked, deboned
   and finely chopped
5 eggs, boiled, finely chopped

1/4 C. cubed pickle (salad cubes)
Celery salt, to taste
Duke's mayonnaise

Combine chopped chicken, chopped eggs, pickle, celery salt and enough mayonnaise to hold mixture together. Chill and serve as sandwich filling or on lettuce leaves.

Note: This recipe is wonderful for tea sandwiches or a picnic.

CONFETTI SALAD

1 med. head Boston lettuce,
   torn in pieces
1 bunch leaf lettuce, torn in pieces
1 bunch Romaine lettuce,
   torn in pieces
4 carrots, thinly sliced
8 radishes, thinly sliced
4 med. tomatoes, cut in 8 wedges

4 green onions and tops, thinly sliced
1 pt. fresh mushrooms, thinly sliced
   (optional)
1 1/2 C. sharp Cheddar cheese, cubed
1 C. summer squash, grated
McCormick Salad Toppings,
   for garnish

In a large bowl (a punch bowl is perfect), place washed and torn lettuce leaves, being sure lettuce is drained well (a salad spinner works wonders). Add remaining ingredients except garnish. Toss to mix ingredients evenly. Garnish with Salad Toppings. Serve with an assortment of salad dressings.

Note: If you wish, salad can be layered beginning with lettuce and alternating the other ingredients with lettuce between each layer. It looks pretty in a large glass bowl either way.

Second Note: A food processor makes short work of slicing the vegetables.

Variation: To make Grilled Chicken Salad, add 6 boneless, skinless chicken breast halves that have been grilled and cut into bite-size pieces.

DILLED CUCUMBERS

3 med. cucumbers, peeled
and sliced thin
1 C. buttermilk
1/4 tsp. salt

1/2 tsp. dillweed
1/8 tsp. fresh ground pepper
1 tsp. lemon juice
2 tsp. onion flakes, toasted

Peel and thinly slice cucumbers. Set aside. Combine remaining ingredients in a bowl. Stir in sliced cucumbers and chill for 1 to 2 hours. Serves 6.

MARINATED GREEN BEAN SALAD

3 lb. fresh green beans, ends trimmed
6 qt. water
2 med.-size red bell peppers, seeded
and cut in thin strips
1 C. finely chopped red onion

2/3 C. Italian dressing
1/2 tsp. salt
1/2 tsp. pepper
1/4 tsp. red pepper flakes

Steam beans and cook in boiling, salted water for 12 to 15 minutes until just tender. Drain. Rinse beans with cold water to stop the cooking process. Drain again. Toss with remaining ingredients and marinate several hours or overnight.

OLD GLORY SALAD

1 bx. blackberry Jell-O
2 bx. raspberry Jell-O
5 C. boiling water
1 C. light cream
1 C. sugar
1 can blueberries with juice

1 env. unflavored gelatin
dissolved in 1/2 C. water
1 tsp. vanilla
1 8-oz. pkg. cream cheese
1/2 C. nutmeats

Dissolve raspberry Jell-O in 4 cups boiling water; pour into 8x12" pan. Chill until firm. Scald cream and sugar; add to unflavored gelatin. Beat in vanilla and cream cheese; add nuts. Pour over raspberry Jell-O. Chill until firm. Dissolve blackberry Jell-O in 1 cup water; add blueberries and juice. Pour over cheese layer. Chill until firm.

PARTY POTATO SALAD

8 to 10 potatoes, peeled and boiled
1 med. onion, chopped
4 hard-cooked eggs
3/4 C. diced celery
1 bell pepper
4 to 6 slices fried bacon, crumbled
3 T. bacon grease

1 T. garlic salt
1/2 T. pepper
1/2 T. celery salt
1/2 T. paprika
1/4 C. vinegar
1 C. mayonnaise
1 C. sour cream

Mix all ingredients together. Refrigerate. Serve cold. Keeps up to 1 week in the refrigerator.

LAYERED TACO SALAD

2 lb. hamburger
2 cans tomato soup
2 cans Ro-Tel tomatoes with chilies
2 cans chili hot beans
1 lb. Velveeta cheese

1 T. chili powder
1 tsp. garlic powder
Salt and pepper
Lettuce, tomatoes and onions
1 lg. pkg. taco chips

Brown hamburger, seasonings and onions. Add soup, Ro-Tel tomatoes and beans; simmer 45 minutes. Layer: Fritos, sauce, cheese, lettuce and tomatoes.

STUFFED TOMATO SALAD

6 med. to lg. tomatoes
2 med. cucumbers,
    chilled and chopped
2 T. chives, chopped finely

1 C. Cream Salad Dressing
Salt and pepper, to taste
Lettuce leaves
Fresh parsley sprigs

Cut a slice from the stem end of each tomato and scoop out pulp. Turn tomatoes upside down on a plate in a cool place. Chop the tomato pulp and add to chopped cucumber; add chopped chives. Stir in 1 cup of Cream Salad Dressing. Salt and pepper to taste. Refill tomatoes, heaping mixture in a mound or pyramid on top. Garnish with parsley sprigs and place each on lettuce leaves.

Cream Salad Dressing:
1 1/2 tsp. salt
1/2 T. mustard
1 T. sugar
1 egg, slightly beaten

2 1/2 C. melted butter or margarine
3/4 C. cream*
4 T. white vinegar

*Evaporated skim milk may be substituted for cream.
Mix ingredients in order listed. Add vinegar a little at a time, beating constantly. Cook in double boiler until mixture thickens; continue beating. Strain at once and chill. Makes approximately 1 1/4 cups.

SWEET 'N SOUR VEGETABLE SALAD
Betty Miller Wilkins - Prosperity, SC

1 12-oz. can French green beans,
    drained
1 can garden peas, drained
1 med. onion, thinly sliced
1 green pepper, thinly sliced
1 C. cider vinegar

1 C. sugar
1/2 C. salad oil
1 tsp. salt
1 jar chopped pimientos
1 tsp. paprika

Mix first 4 ingredients together. Mix remaining ingredients and add to first mixture. Better when made 24 hours ahead. Serves 8.
Keeps several days.

- BREADS -

BISCUIT CRESCENT BREAD

2 8-oz. cans refrigerated biscuits   4 tsp. sesame seeds
1 egg white, beaten slightly

Preheat oven to 350°. Open biscuits (do not separate biscuits). Place the biscuits in a roll (stand on edge and place end to end) on an ungreased cookie sheet. Press together slightly to make one long loaf. Press ends in and down slightly; bend into crescent shape. Brush with egg white. Sprinkle with sesame seeds. Bake approximately 25 minutes at 350° until golden brown.

CHEESE BREAD

1 (13 3/4-oz.) pkg. hot roll mix   1 tsp. paprika
1 egg   2 C. sharp Cheddar cheese, grated
A few grains cayenne pepper

In large bowl, following package directions, prepare hot roll mix, using 3/4 cup warm (not hot) water and 1 egg. Stir in cayenne and paprika. Cover with damp tea towel and let rise in warm place (80 to 85°) until doubled in bulk (approximately 35 to 45 minutes). Turn dough out on lightly floured board and knead for about 5 minutes. Dough should be smooth and elastic. Roll out on floured surface into an 8x15" rectangle. Sprinkle cheese on dough. Roll up tightly, starting with 8" side as you would a jelly-roll. Pinch edges together. Place in a greased 9x5" loaf pan with seam against side (not bottom) of pan. Let rise, covered in a warm place for 30 to 45 minutes. Preheat oven to 375° and bake for 60 to 65 minutes. Crust should be brown and sound hollow when you "thump" it with your knuckle. Cool on a wire rack. Slice.
Note: Good for sandwiches too!

FRENCH ONION BREAD

1 lg. loaf French bread   1/2 pkg. dry onion soup mix
1/4 C. butter or margarine, melted

Slice bread diagonally 1/2" thick (not cutting through bottom). Brush top and sides with melted butter; sprinkle with dry onion soup. Wrap in foil; heat on grill until hot (approximately 20 minutes). Serve by cutting or breaking off slices.
Note: One-half cup grated Cheddar cheese mixed with 1 teaspoon chili powder may be substituted for the onion soup mix. This is also very good for barbecues. Both breads may be baked in a conventional oven as well.

Biscuit dough cut in desired shapes makes perfect dumplings. Just drop into boiling broth from chicken, cover and cook 12 minutes without uncovering.

. . . hearts go home for the holidays

- SIDE DISHES -

BAKED BEANS

32 oz. pork and beans
1/2 C. dark brown sugar
1/2 C. minced onion or
    1 1/2 T. dry onion soup mix
3/4 lb. hot sausage (bulk)

1/2 tsp. dry mustard
1/2 tsp. prepared mustard
1/2 C. catsup
1 T. Worcestershire sauce

Fry sausage in patties. Drain and crumble with fork. Set aside. Combine remaining ingredients. Add sausage. Stir and pour into 9x13" casserole dish. Bake at 350° for 1 to 1½ hours. Serves 6 to 8.

SWEET & SOUR BLACK-EYE PEAS

1 lb. cooked and drained black-eye
    peas or 2 1-lb. cans
1/4 C. cane syrup or molasses
1/4 C. cider vinegar

1 tsp. dry mustard
1 tsp. garlic powder
4 pineapple slices
Brown sugar

Combine black-eye peas, syrup, vinegar, mustard and garlic powder. Pour mixture into a shallow 2-quart casserole dish. Top with pineapple slices. Sprinkle with brown sugar. Bake at 375° for 40 minutes. Serves 8.

BOILED CORN ON THE COB

6 ears corn (fresh or frozen)
Boiling water, to cover 1 1/2"
1 1/2 tsp. sugar or 1 pkg. Sweet 'N Low

Butter, salt and pepper, to taste
    (when serving)

If using fresh corn, remove husks and silks. Rinse corn in cold water. Bring water and sugar to a rolling boil in large pot. Break fresh ears of corn in half; place in boiling water. Boil for 6 to 7 minutes or until tender. Do not add salt while cooking (salt tends to toughen corn). When done, drain water. Serve immediately with lots of butter and salt and pepper to taste.

Great with fried chicken.

ROASTED CORN ON THE COB

Aluminum foil
1 doz. ears fresh yellow corn

2 tsp. butter or margarine
    (per ear of corn)

Remove husks and silks from corn. Place each ear on a separate piece of foil (cut large enough to wrap and seal each). Place 2 teaspoons butter on each ear. Wrap and seal corn. Bake in a preheated 400° oven for 25 to 30 minutes. Place foil-wrapped, hot corn on a large platter. Place butter, salt and pepper by platter for serving.

Note: Use as many ears of corn as you need for this recipe. May be cooked over hot coals on a grill as well for cookouts.

ROASTED CORN IN HUSKS (ON GRILL)

8 ears of corn (or number you need)   Aluminum foil
Ice water

Peel outer husks back just enough to remove silks from ear of corn (keep stem end husks and corn intact). Replace husks around corn and drop into large container of ice water. When ready to cook, remove from ice water and wrap in aluminum foil. Seal tightly. Roast for 25 to 30 minutes over or in hot coals.

Delicious and pretty!

HASH BROWN CASSEROLE

2 (2-lb.) pkg. frozen hash brown   1 1/2 C. sour cream
   potatoes, thawed slightly   1 stick butter or margarine, melted
1 C. onion, chopped (3 green onions   1 tsp. salt
   and tender tops are best)   1 tsp. pepper (freshly ground
1 can cream of chicken soup   if possible)
12 oz. sharp Cheddar cheese, grated

Mix all ingredients. Pour into large buttered casserole dish. Sprinkle Topping over and bake at 300° for 1 hour. Serves 10 to 12.

Topping:
1 1/2 to 2 C. crushed potato chips or
   1 can French fried onion rings

Note: This dish is good with ham, beef or poultry.

POTATO CHIPS

Seasoned coating mix for chicken   3 to 4 lg. potatoes, boiled (whole)
   (Shake 'N Bake brand)   1/2 C. margarine or oil

Chill boiled potatoes. Slice into 1/4" thick slices. Coat with seasoned mix. Brown in hot margarine or oil until crispy brown. Drain on paper towels. Serve hot. Serves 4.

VEG-ALL CASSEROLE

2 cans Veg-All mixed vegetables,   1 can sliced water chestnuts, drained
   drained   1 C. sharp Cheddar cheese, grated
1 med. onion, minced fine   1 C. Hellmann's mayonnaise

Mix drained vegetables and water chestnuts with remaining ingredients. Pour into a buttered 9x13" casserole dish. Bake at 350° for 20 to 25 minutes. Add Topping. Return to oven and bake until Topping is lightly browned. Makes 6 to 8 servings.

Topping: Or:
1 1/2 C. crushed croutons mixed with   1 1/2 C. crushed potato chips
   1/4 C. melted margarine,

- MAIN DISHES -

FIREWORKS PIE

1 11-oz. can jalapeno peppers   4 eggs, beaten
8 oz. sharp Cheddar cheese, grated

Drain peppers, remove seeds. Slice peppers into thin strips and place in bottom of greased pie plate. Spread cheese over peppers. Pour beaten eggs over cheese. Bake at 325° for 45 to 50 minutes. Cool 25 to 30 minutes. Slice and serve with plenty of something cold to drink!

BARBECUED CHICKEN

Sauce:
Use Uncle Hammond's Barbecue Sauce (see Table of Contents - 4th of July: Main Dishes).

Grill Cooked:
Brown 2 1/2 to 3 pound cut up chicken on grill over medium heat fire. Place chicken on 2 layers of heavy duty foil. Spread Sauce evenly over chicken, seal tightly. Place foil pocket on grill; cook 30 minutes.

Oven Cooked:
Heat oven to 375°. Arrange 2 1/2 to 3 pound cut up chicken in 12x8" baking dish. Spread Sauce evenly over chicken; cover with foil. Bake at 375° for 30 minutes. Remove foil and bake uncovered an additional 30 to 35 minutes.

BLUSHING CHICKEN

6 boneless, skinless   1/4 C. olive oil
   chicken breast halves   2 tsp. butter or margarine
1 tsp. seasoned salt   1 1/2 C. milk
1/4 C. flour   4 T. sour cream
1 T. paprika

In a shallow bowl, mix flour and paprika. Salt the chicken and roll in flour mixture. Place olive oil and butter in a skillet. Brown chicken on both sides. Reduce heat. Add milk; cover and simmer 25 to 30 minutes. When ready to serve, remove from heat and stir in sour cream.

CELEBRATION CHICKEN

1 whole chicken   1/2 C. soy sauce
1/3 C. frozen orange juice concentrate   1 tsp. lemon juice
   (undiluted)   1/4 tsp. red pepper flakes

Marinate chicken in last 4 ingredients for 4 to 6 hours. Turn several times. Bake at 400° for 1½ hours. Baste several times with marinade.

PICNIC FRIED CHICKEN

1 (3 to 4-lb.) chicken
Salt and pepper, to taste
1 tsp. garlic salt (optional)
1 tsp. thyme

1 tsp. paprika
1 C. buttermilk
1 C. flour or 1 1/2 C. self-rising flour
2 C. corn oil or 1 C. shortening

Cut chicken into serving pieces; wash and dry on paper towel. In paper bag combine flour, salt, pepper, garlic salt, thyme and paprika. Dip chicken in buttermilk, then shake in flour mixture in paper bag. Heat oil to 275 to 350°. Add chicken; cook until golden brown, turning once. Drain on paper towel. Arrange on platter; garnish with parsley, if desired.

May use leftover buttermilk to make gravy.

Note: The secret to good fried chicken is to have the chicken cold and the oil hot.

GULF SHRIMP

1/2 C. soy sauce or teriyaki sauce
12 lg. shrimp, raw, peeled, tails left on

6 strips bacon

Marinate shrimp in soy or teriyaki sauce for 1 hour. Partially cook bacon, cut each strip in half. Wrap bacon around raw shrimp. Broil or grill until bacon is crisp, turning to cook evenly. Serves 4.

HAMBURGER DELUXE

2 lb. ground chuck
2 T. prepared mustard
2 T. catsup

1 T. minced onion (optional) or
   2 tsp. prepared horseradish
   (optional)

Lightly mix ground chuck with other ingredients. Shape into 8 equal patties. Grill 4" from hot coals (about 4 minutes for medium-rare or cook until desired doneness). Serve with heated buns, condiments, lettuce, tomato and onions.

Note: For cheeseburgers, add a slice of cheese about 4 minutes before hamburgers are done.

MARINATED STEAK ON THE GRILL

1/4 C. soy sauce
2 T. vinegar
3 T. honey
1 1/2 tsp. garlic chips

1 1/2 tsp. ground ginger
3/4 C. vegetable oil
6 steaks

Mix all ingredients and pour over meat. Refrigerate at least overnight. Grill over very hot coals 5 minutes on each side or until desired doneness. Yield: 6 servings.

Note: This marinade works well on any cut of steak and on London Broil.

To prevent breaded meats from losing their coating, bread 20 to 30 minutes
ahead and let rest on wax paper until ready to fry.

. . . hearts go home for the holidays

BOURBON BARBECUED BABY BACK RIBS

1 rack baby back ribs,
   cut in serving pieces

Salt and pepper

Cut ribs into desired number of servings. Salt and pepper ribs. Grill 5 minutes on bottom sides without Sauce. Thereafter, baste with Sauce and grill for approximately 15 more minutes. Turn several times during grilling to cook evenly on both sides. Serve with lots of napkins, corn on the cob and coleslaw.

Sauce:
1 T. olive oil
1 med. size onion, thinly sliced
3 T. good bourbon whiskey
1 tsp. dried thyme or
   1 T. chopped fresh

1 tsp. rosemary
1/2 C. barbecue sauce, bottled
   (your favorite brand)

In a heavy skillet, saute onions in oil for 5 minutes over medium heat; add thyme, rosemary and bourbon. Simmer for 2 minutes. Stir in bottled barbecue sauce.

GRILLED SAUSAGES, PEPPERS AND ONIONS

2 lb. Hillshire Farms
   smoked sausage links

Barbecue sauce, bottled
   (your favorite brand)
1 sm. onion, minced

Cut sausage into desired lengths. Score links a few times with knife. Combine barbecue sauce and onion. Pour over sausage links. Marinate for 2 or 3 hours. Drain (reserve sauce). Baste with sauce. Grill until browned, 4 or 5 minutes on each side.

UNCLE HAMMOND'S BARBECUE SAUCE
(A Secret for 30 Years)
Hammond Ferguson - Lincolnton, GA
(Husband of Joann McCurry Ferguson - One of the Twelve)

1 gal. Twelve Oaks distilled vinegar
1 C. sugar
3 T. black pepper
1 C. Worcestershire sauce

2 T. red hot pepper (cayenne)
3 T. salt
2 sticks butter
4 32-oz. bot. ketchup

Combine all ingredients and bring to rolling boil. Reduce heat and cook for 1 hour. Use when barbecuing chicken or pork. Good on beef too.

For barbecued chicken, omit ketchup; for pork, omit Worcestershire sauce.

Cook tough cuts of meat (roasts, etc.) in strong tea.

Spray broiling pan rack with non-stick cooking spray. Have broiler and broiling rack hot before placing meat on it.

- DESSERTS -

BANANA SPLIT CAKE (NO BAKING REQUIRED)

1/2 C. butter, melted
2 1/2 C. graham cracker crumbs
2 T. granulated sugar
1/2 C. butter, softened
2 C. powdered sugar
2 eggs, beaten
1 #2 can crushed pineapple, drained

3 bananas, sliced
2 10-oz. pkg. frozen strawberries,
  drained
2 C. whipped cream
1/2 C. chopped nuts
20 maraschino cherries

Combine melted butter, crumbs and sugar; pat into 9x13" pan. Beat together the softened butter, powdered sugar and eggs; spread over crumbs. Pour drained pineapple over powdered sugar mixture. Layer with sliced bananas and strawberries. Spread whipped cream over fruits, then sprinkle with nuts. Top each serving with a cherry. Chill until firm. Slice in squares and serve on chilled dessert plates. Yield: 20 servings.

PEANUT BUTTER FILLED CUPCAKES

1 chocolate cake mix
1/2 C. crunchy-style peanut butter
1 8-oz. pkg. cream cheese, softened

2 T. honey
2 T. milk

Prepare cake mix according to package directions; fill cupcake paper liners 2/3 full with batter. Combine remaining ingredients; drop a teaspoonful into each cupcake. Bake at 350° for 30 minutes. Makes 1 1/2 to 2 dozen.

PUNCH BOWL DESSERT

1 lg. angel food cake or 2 loaf size
1 lg. bx. vanilla instant pudding
1 can blueberry pie filling or
  any pie filling

1 lg. pkg. or 2 sm. pkg. whipped
  topping mix

Prepare whipped topping as per directions. Refrigerate. Prepare instant pudding as per directions. Set aside. Tear cake into small pieces. In a small punch bowl, arrange a layer of cake on bottom. Spread a layer of pudding over cake. Spread a layer of whipped topping over pudding. Repeat layering. Top with pie filling of choice. Chill for 6 hours or overnight. Scoop into sherbet glasses. Garnish with fresh whole strawberries made into fans.

Note: To make strawberry "fan", hold medium to large strawberry stem end with fingers. Turn strawberry on its side. Make cut with a sharp knife through middle (from top to bottom - do not cut through stem); then make cuts on both sides of middle cut (making thin still attached slices). Lightly press stem end between thumb and forefinger and fan out slices. These are pretty for garnishing.

SHORTCAKE I

2 C. flour
4 tsp. baking powder
1/2 tsp. salt

2 tsp. sugar
1/4 C. butter (1/2 stick)
3/4 C. milk

Preheat oven to 400°. Combine dry ingredients in a large bowl; cut in butter with pastry blender; add milk gradually. Turn out on lightly floured board; toss lightly. Divide dough into two parts. Pat out 1/4" thick and cut with biscuit cutter. Bake for 12 minutes at 400°. Using 2 each, put sweetened berries (strawberries or blueberries) between layers and on top. Put whipped cream on top layer of berries.

SHORTCAKE BISCUITS

2 C. all-purpose flour
1/4 C. plus 2 tsp. granulated sugar
1 T. baking powder

1/2 tsp. salt
1 C. whipping cream

Sift flour, sugar, baking powder and salt together into a large bowl. Stir in cream, a little at a time, with a fork. Mix only until dough is lumpy. Knead gently 1 or 2 times and roll into a roll about 6" long. Slice in 6 even pieces. Bake in a preheated 400° oven on a greased cookie sheet for 15 minutes. Cool 8 to 10 minutes.

Slice each half with a bread or serrated knife. Place desired Filling on bottom half. Place top half over Filling. Put whipped cream and some of Filling on top.

Fillings:
Approx. 12 oz. sweetened strawberries
Approx. 12 oz. sweetened blueerries

Approx. 12 oz. sweetened peaches
Sweetened whipped cream, for topping

CHERRY BLUEBERRY CHEESE PIE
(RED, WHITE AND BLUE)

1 9" graham cracker crust
1 8-oz. pkg. cream cheese, softened
1 14-oz. can sweetened
    condensed milk
1/3 C. lemon juice

1 tsp. vanilla
1/2 of 21-oz. can cherry pie filling,
    chilled
1/2 of 21-oz. can blueberry pie filling,
    chilled

Using an electric mixer in a large bowl, beat cheese until light and fluffy. Pour milk in a little at a time and mix until smooth. Add lemon juice and vanilla. Mix until well blended. Pour into graham cracker crust. Chill 3 to 4 hours. Put chilled blueberry pie filling on the top in center (about the size of a saucer). Place cherry pie filling around blueberry filling to edges. If pie filling is too runny, you may want to drain it a little before topping pie. Pipe whipped cream in the shape of a star in the center or simply top individual slices with whipped cream. Refrigerate any leftovers.

Note: Use leftover pie fillings over ice cream.

RITZY STRAWBERRY PIE

Crust:

23 Ritz crackers, broken in
   small pieces
1 C. pecans, coarsely chopped

3 egg whites
1 tsp. vanilla
1 C. sugar

Beat egg whites until stiff. Add sugar and continue beating until well mixed. Fold in other ingredients. Bake in well-greased pie plate for 30 minutes at 350°. Allow to cool thoroughly.

Pie Filling:

1 lg. pkg. frozen strawberries, well
   drained or 1 qt. fresh strawberries,
   sweetened to taste and well drained

1 C. whipping cream
2 tsp. sugar

Whip cream until stiff. Add sugar and beat until well mixed. Fold in strawberries. Pour into cold pie crust. Refrigerate 2 hours before serving. Garnish with fresh strawberries.

BUTTERMILK FUDGE

1/2 C. butter (no substitute)
2 C. granulated sugar
2 T. light corn syrup

1 tsp. baking soda
1 C. buttermilk
1 C. chopped pecans

Combine all ingredients except nuts in a large heavy saucepan. Cook on medium heat until a very small amount of mixture (1/4 teaspoon) dropped in a bowl of cold water forms a soft ball. At this point, beat hot mixture until creamy. Fold in pecans. Pour into a buttered shallow pan. Cool until firm and cut into 1" squares.

BASIC BROWNIES

4 C. sugar
1 C. flour
1 C. cocoa
8 eggs

1 lb. butter, melted
4 tsp. vanilla
2 C. chopped nuts

Sift sugar, flour and cocoa together. Beat eggs well; add sifted dry ingredients, butter, vanilla and nuts, mixing well. Pour into a 13x9" pan. Set a larger, shallow pan containing hot water on lowest oven shelf. Place the batter pan in the pan of hot water. Bake at 300° for 45 to 50 minutes. Brownies will firm while cooling. Yield: 3 dozen.

NO BAKE BROWNIES

1 12-oz. pkg. semi-sweet
  chocolate morsels
1 14-oz. can sweetened
  condensed milk

1 (8 1/2-oz.) pkg. chocolate wafers,
  finely crushed
1 C. chopped nuts, divided

Melt over hot (not boiling) water, chocolate morsels; stir until smooth*. Add sweetened condensed milk, chocolate wafer crumbs and 1/2 cup nuts; stir until well blended. Press into foil-lined 8" square pan. Press remaining 1/2 cup nuts into top of brownie. Let stand at room temperature until firm. Cut into 2" squares. Makes sixteen 2" brownies.

*In microwave: melt on High for 1 minute; stir. Repeat.

B. J.'S LEMON BARS
Betty Miller Wilkins - Prosperity, SC

Crust:

1 C. margarine, softened
2 C. plain flour

1/2 C. confectioner's sugar

Cream margarine, flour and sugar; press into 9x13" pan. Bake at 350° for 20 minutes.

Topping:

4 eggs, beaten
2 C. sugar (granulated)
1 tsp. salt

1 tsp. baking powder
6 T. lemon juice
3 T. plain flour

While Crust is baking, make Topping as follows: Mix beaten eggs, sugar and salt. Beat well. Add baking powder, lemon juice and flour. Mix well. Spread Topping on Crust and bake for 30 to 40 minutes more. Cool slightly and dust with confectioner's sugar. When cool, cut in squares.

PEACH ICE CREAM

1 14-oz. can sweetened
  condensed milk
4 whole eggs, beaten
1 C. sugar

6 C. milk
1 qt. mashed peaches (pre-sweetened)
1 tsp. almond flavoring
Pinch of salt

Mix together and freeze in ice cream freezer/churn. Makes 1 gallon.

FROZEN STRAWBERRY SQUARES

1 C. flour
1/4 C. brown sugar
1/4 C. chopped nuts
1/2 C. melted butter
2 egg whites

1 lg. ctn. whipped topping
1/2 C. sugar
2 T. lemon juice
2 C. fresh strawberries

Mix first 4 ingredients; spread crumbs into 8x8" pan. Bake at 325° for 20 minutes. Stir occasionally. Cool. Pack 2/3 of crumbs in pan for crust. Beat egg whites and sugar. Mix in whipped topping, lemon juice and crushed strawberries. Pour over crumbs. Sprinkle rest of crumbs on top. Cover. Freeze 3 to 6 hours. Cut in squares to serve. Garnish with strawberry fan or whole strawberry.

WATERMELON WITH SHERRY SAUCE

1 med. watermelon

Sprigs of mint

Scoop balls from melon center. Set aside covered in refrigerator while you make Sauce. Pour Sauce over melon balls and let stand covered in refrigerator. Serve in champagne flutes. Garnish with sprigs of mint.

Sauce:
1 C. granulated sugar
1/4 C. water
1/2 C. dry sherry

3 T. Sloe gin
Dash salt

Cook sugar and water in a saucepan for 3 minutes over medium heat. Cool slightly; add sherry, Sloe gin and salt. Chill.

Halloween

- PARTY FOODS -

BAKED CARAMEL CORN

2 sticks margarine
2 C. firmly packed brown sugar
1/2 C. light corn syrup
1 tsp. salt

1/2 tsp. baking soda
1 tsp. vanilla
6 qt. popped popcorn

Melt butter; stir in brown sugar, corn syrup and salt. Bring to boil, stirring constantly; boil without stirring 5 minutes. Remove from heat; stir in soda and vanilla. Gradually pour over popped corn, mixing well. Turn into large pan. You may need two. Use 1 of the largest aluminum foil pans you can buy. Bake in 250° oven for 1 hour, stirring every 15 minutes. Remove from oven; cool completely. Break apart and store in tightly covered container.

CRISP SUGARED NUTS

1 egg white
1 rounded tsp. salt
1 tsp. milk

1 tsp. water
1/2 tsp. sugar
2 C. nuts (pecans or walnuts halves)

Dip nuts in mix and bake for 15 minutes at 250°. Turn oven off and let pecans remain in oven for 30 minutes more.

TOASTED PUMPKIN/SQUASH SEEDS

Seeds from lg. pumpkin or
    acorn squash, dried
1/2 stick butter

1 or 2 tsp. seasoned salt
A few grains of cayenne

Saute pumpkin seeds in butter; add seasonings. Spread on cookie sheet lined with brown paper. Bake at 250° until crisp. Stir often. Watch carefully to prevent overcooking. Cool and enjoy.
Variation: Melt butter in bottom of jelly-roll pan. Add seeds and stir, coating both sides. Sprinkle with salt and bake at 250° until crisp.

Slice a little of the white off the bottom of a boiled egg to make it lie flat. This works for anything rounded on the bottom that you may serve.

PIGS IN A BLANKET

1 15-oz. pkg. refrigerated ready
    to bake pie crusts for 9" pie
3/4 to 1 lb. cocktail frankfurters
    (Hillshire Farm brand)

Mustard (hot or plain)
1 egg, beaten in 1 T. water

Place pie crust dough on a flat surface. Using a pizza cutter, cut one piece to use as a pattern for the rest. Pieces need to be large enough to wrap the frank and overlap just a bit. Place each frank on a piece of dough. Brush each frank with mustard. Pinch all the seams together. Place on a lightly greased cookie sheet about 1" apart. Brush tops and sides with egg/water mixture. Bake in a preheated 425° oven for 12 to 14 minutes or until crisp and golden brown. Makes approximately 36.

SAUSAGE BISCUIT BAKE

1 1-lb. pkg. Jimmy Dean sausage
1 C. flour
3 tsp. baking powder
1/2 tsp. salt
3 T. solid shortening
    (preferably Crisco)

1/2 C. buttermilk or milk
1/4 tsp. cracked black pepper or
    ground black pepper
1/2 C. grated Cheddar cheese

In a 9x9" casserole dish, press the sausage out to cover bottom. In a bowl, combine flour, baking powder and salt; cut in shortening with a fork or pastry cutter until dough is crumbly. Pour in milk, cheese, and pepper, stirring until you have a soft dough. Knead a few times and roll out dough. Knead a few times and roll out to 9x9". Place on top of sausage. Bake at 450° for 10 to 14 minutes. Drain off any excess drippings from sausage. Makes 4 to 6 servings.

WITCH'S HAT CENTER PIECE

1 (12 to 18") styrofoam cone
1 sheet black poster board
Black licorice rope candy
Toothpicks
3 bunches endive

2 lb. fresh or frozen shrimp
    with tails on
Baby carrots (optional)
Cocktail tomatoes (optional)

Boil, peel and devein shrimp. Season to taste. Cover cone with black paper or black poster board and attach with florist pins or toothpick halves. Cut a circle wider than the base of the cone; attach to bottom of cone with florist pins or toothpick halves. Or cut out the center of the circle and slide it down over the cone to the bottom to resemble brim of witch's hat. Tie three licorice ropes around the base of the cone to make the hat band. Tie licorice in a bow. Starting at the base of the cone, cover the cone with over-lapping leaves of endive and attach to cone with florist pins or toothpick halves or simply use with just the paper or poster board. Starting at the bottom, attach boiled shrimp, and/or cocktail tomatoes and/or baby carrots to the cone with toothpicks.

Note: Cubes of cheese, ham, olives, etc. may be used to "decorate" your hat or use your imagination in creating this centerpiece.

DIP FOR APPLES

1 12-oz. pkg. butterscotch morsels
1 14-oz. can condensed milk

1 1/2 tsp. cinnamon
1 T. white vinegar

Mix all ingredients in 2-quart saucepan (in a pan of water). Cook on medium heat until smooth.

GOLDEN DIP

1 pt. mayonnaise
1 1/2 C. buttermilk
1/2 tsp. seasoned salt
1/2 tsp. cracked pepper
  (or freshly ground)

1/2 tsp. Accent
1/2 tsp. garlic powder
1/2 tsp. lemon pepper
1/2 tsp. onion powder

Stir ingredients together. Refrigerate until ready to use. Keeps for 2 to 3 weeks. Serve in Pumpkin Shell.
Good dip for anything. Great on salads too!

Pumpkin Shells for Dip:
2 sm. pie pumpkins
Sharp knife

Tablespoon
Lemon juice

Cut top of pumpkin about 1 1/2" down. Scrape seeds, etc., out of inside with spoon. Rub cut edges of top and inside with lemon juice. Fill with dips (hot or cold). Place on a bed of autumn leaves. Put tops back on until ready to serve.
See Table of Contents for Dips.
Note: Large regular pumpkin can be hollowed out and used for punch "bowls".

PARTY CHEESE BALL

12 oz. cream cheese
4 oz. blue cheese
1 stick butter

1 3-oz. can black olives,
  chopped and drained
1/2 C. chopped nuts (any kind
  of nuts will do)

Mix softened cream cheese, blue cheese and butter until blended. Fold in drained, chopped black olives. Mold into a ball or rectangle and roll in chopped nuts. Chill until 30 minutes before ready to serve. Serve with assorted crackers. Enough for a crowd.

HAYSTACK SPREAD

4 C. finely chopped ham
1 8-oz. pkg. cream cheese
3/4 C. salad dressing

1/3 C. green onion slices
1/4 C. pickle relish
Blanched slivered almonds, toasted

Combine ham, 4 ounces softened cream cheese, 1/2 cup salad dressing, 1/2 cup toasted slivered almonds (chop before adding), onion and pickle relish. Mix well; chill. Shape into 1 large or 2 small cone-shaped mounds. Combine 1/4 cup of salad dressing and remaining cream cheese; mix well. Frost mound with cream cheese mixture. Chill slightly; cover with toasted slivered almonds. Serve with crackers or party rye bread, if desired.

- BEVERAGES -

WITCH'S BREW

2 qt. apple cider
1/2 C. brown sugar
1/4 tsp. salt
1 stick cinnamon

1 tsp. whole allspice
1 tsp. whole cloves
Orange slices, for garnish

In a saucepan, mix cider, sugar, salt and spices. Heat until just before boiling point. Reduce heat to low. Cover and simmer 20 to 25 minutes. Serve hot in mugs. Garnish with orange slices. Makes 2 quarts.

HALLOWEEN EGGNOG

6 eggs, separated
1/2 C. sugar
2 C. milk

2 C. whipping cream
1 C. frozen orange juice
concentrate, undiluted

In large mixing bowl, combine egg yolks, sugar, milk, whipping cream and orange juice concentrate. Beat with rotary beaters until thickened and foamy. Chill. In bowl, beat egg whites until stiff, but not dry. Gently fold into orange mixture. Serve immediately in chilled punch cups. Garnish with grated orange rind. Yield: 24 (1/2 cup) servings.

Note: May be served from medium-sized seeded pumpkin. Put dry ice and water in small containers around pumpkin for "spooky" look. (This can be done with any Halloween punch.)

HALLOWEEN PUNCH

6 lg. oranges
1 pt. cranberry juice
1 12-oz. can apricot nectar
1/4 C. lemon juice

1/4 C. sugar
Paper cupcake liners
1 12-oz. bot. ginger ale, chilled
6 drinking straws, halved crosswise

With a sharp knife, cut a 1/2" thick slice from one end of each orange. Scoop out pulp, to leave a hollow orange shell; reserve pulp. With black wax crayon, draw a face on each orange shell. Set aside. Press reserved orange pulp through strainer, to extract enough of the juice to measure 1 cup. In large bowl, combine orange juice with cranberry juice, apricot nectar, lemon juice, and sugar; mix well. Refrigerate at least 1 hour or until serving.

To serve: Line each orange shell with 2 paper cupcake liners, one inside the other. Add ginger ale to fruit mixture; mix well. Pour punch into orange cups. Serve each with 2 straw halves. Paper cupcake liners and straws can be discarded and replaced with new ones, and same orange shell used for serving another person. Makes 25 (2-ounce) servings.

HARVEST PUNCH

1 qt. cranberry juice cocktail
1 46-oz. can pineapple juice
1 46-oz. can fruit punch　.

1 qt. ginger ale
Orange and lemon slices

Chill ingredients overnight in refrigerator. Open and pour over ice ring or ice cubes in large punch bowl. Garnish with orange and lemon slices to float on top. Makes 35 servings.

ORANGE SANGRIA

1 orange
1/4 C. sugar
2 C. orange juice

1 (25.4-oz.) bot. Burgundy, chilled
1/2 C. Triple Sec or other
    orange-flavored liqueur

Slice orange in half. Cut 1 half into 3 slices. Quarter each slice and reserve for garnish. Carefully cut off the thin outer peel of the other half with a vegetable peeler. Combine orange peel and sugar in bowl. Mash peel with a spoon. Stir in remaining ingredients; cover and chill for 15 minutes. Remove peel and serve over ice. Serves 6 to 8.

For beer batter, use equal parts of beer and flour. Let stand 3 hours at room temperature.

- SOUPS -

MICROWAVE CHEESE/BEER SOUP

1 sm. onion, chopped
1/4 C. margarine or butter
1/3 C. all-purpose flour
1 T. instant chicken bouillon
3 1/2 C. milk

1 8-oz. jar pasteurized
  process cheese spread
1 C. shredded Cheddar cheese
  (about 4-oz.)
1 C. beer

Cover and microwave onion and margarine in 2-quart casserole dish on High until onion is tender, 3 to 4 minutes. Stir in flour and bouillon, then gradually stir in milk. Cover and microwave to boiling, 3 to 5 minutes. Stir in cheese spread, cheese and beer. Cover and microwave until hot and bubbly and cheese is melted, 3 to 4 minutes; stir. Makes 5 to 6 servings.

CROCK POT CHILI

1 1/2 lb. browned ground beef
3/4 lb. bacon, cooked and chopped
1 C. chopped onion
2 15-oz. cans pork and beans
1 15-oz. can kidney beans, drained
1 15-oz. can tomatoes,
  mashed with fork

1 tsp. Tabasco sauce
1 C. ketchup
1/4 C. brown sugar
1 T. Liquid Smoke
3 T. white vinegar
1 tsp. salt
Dash pepper

Brown and drain ground beef. Put into crock pot. Brown bacon and onion and drain. Add bacon, onion and remaining ingredients to crock pot. Stir well. Cover and cook on low 4 to 9 hours. Serve with Chili Pepper Cornbread (see Table of Contents - Halloween: Breads).

HAM CHOWDER

2 C. diced cooked ham
3/4 C. celery, chopped
1/2 C. chopped onion
1/2 C. butter or margarine
3 10-oz. pkg. frozen cream-style corn,
  thawed

1 C. Half and Half or milk
1/2 tsp. celery salt
1/2 tsp. onion salt
1/2 tsp. pepper
1/2 tsp. hickory salt

Saute ham, celery and onion in butter in a heavy Dutch oven. Stir in cream-style corn, Half and Half or milk, celery salt, onion salt, pepper and hickory salt. Reduce heat and simmer for 20 minutes. Makes about 6 cups.

Leftover gravy freezes well. Add to soups and stews.

. . . hearts go home for the holidays

- SALADS -

SAWDUST SALAD (LAYERED)

First Layer:
1 sm. pkg. lemon Jell-O
1 sm. pkg. orange Jell-O
1 #2 can crushed pineapple, drained
2 bananas, chopped

Miniature marshmallows
2 C. hot water
1 1/2 C. cold water

Dissolve both packages of Jell-O in 2 cups hot water and add 1 1/2 cups cold water. Chill until syrupy, add the drained pineapple and chopped bananas. Place in 9x13" glass casserole dish. Sprinkle miniature marshmallows over top. Chill.

Second Layer:
1 1/2 C. pineapple juice (12-oz.)
1 T. lemon juice
1 1/2 C. sugar
3 T. flour

2 eggs
1 env. plain gelatin
1/2 C. cold water

Soften gelatin in cold water and set aside. Cook pineapple juice, lemon juice, sugar, flour and eggs until thickened. Add the gelatin. Cool and pour over first layer.

Third Layer:
1/2 pt. whipping cream (1 C.)
1 8-oz. pkg. cream cheese, softened

Sharp grated yellow cheese

Whip whipping cream and cream cheese together. Spread on top of salad. Sprinkle over this some grated cheese. Refrigerate until set. Serves 12 to 15.

SWEET AND SOUR CABBAGE

1 cabbage (red or white)
Salt and pepper
2 tart apples, sliced
2 T. shortening or fat

2 T. flour
4 T. brown sugar
2 T. vinegar

Shred the cabbage fine; add salt and pepper to taste and the apples. Heat fat in large skillet; add cabbage and apples. Add boiling water to cover and cook until tender; sprinkle with flour; add sugar and vinegar. Simmer 10 minutes; serve hot.

SWEET AND SOUR SAUERKRAUT

1/4 C. butter
1 lg. onion, chopped

3 T. brown sugar
1 (1-lb. 13-oz.) can sauerkraut

Brown butter; add onion and saute for a few minutes. Add sugar and sauerkraut. Simmer until thoroughly heated.

TURTLE SALAD

1 #303 can pear halves, drained
(reserve juice)
Pecan halves
Lg. stuffed green olives

Lettuce leaves
2 or 3 drops green food coloring
Pistachio Cheese Ball*

*See Table of Contents - St. Patrick's Day: Party Foods.

Drain pears. Reserve juice. Set aside. Put juice in a small mixing bowl; add green food coloring. Place pear halves in juice. Turn several times to color. Drain on paper towels. Place lettuce leaves on individual salad plates (as many as you have pear halves). Place Pistachio Cheese Ball on each lettuce leaf. Place colored pear half, pitted side down, over cheese ball. Arrange 4 pecan halves like "turtle's" feet. Stick a toothpick through large green stuffed olive and attach to pear half for "head". Looks just like a little green turtle!

- BREADS -

BUNDT BREAD

1 C. (4-oz.) shredded Cheddar cheese
1/4 C. butter or margarine, softened
1/2 tsp. Italian seasoning
1/4 tsp. garlic or onion powder
1/4 C. sesame seeds
2 1/2 C. all-purpose flour
2 T. sugar

1 tsp. salt
2 pkg. dry yeast
1/2 C. milk
1/2 C. water
1/4 C. butter or margarine
1 egg

Combine first 4 ingredients; mix until smooth. Set aside. Generously grease a 10" Bundt pan; sprinkle sesame seeds evenly in pan, coating well. Set aside. Combine 1 1/2 cups flour, sugar, salt, and yeast in large mixing bowl; mix well. Combine milk, water, and butter in small saucepan; cook over low heat until mixture reaches 120° on a thermometer, stirring constantly. Add warm milk mixture and egg to flour mixture. Beat at low speed of an electric mixer until moistened; continue beating at medium speed 3 minutes. Gradually stir in remaining 1 cup flour. Pour half of batter evenly into pan, spreading to cover bottom of pan. Spoon cheese filling evenly over batter; top with remaining batter, spreading evenly. Cover pan with plastic wrap; let rise in warm place (85°) for 1 hour or until batter rises 1" from top of pan. Bake at 350° for 35 to 40 minutes.

Note: This looks like a pumpkin. Surround with autumn leaves.

HERBED FRENCH BREAD

Loaf of French bread
1/2 C. soft butter or margarine
1 tsp. parsley flakes
1/4 tsp. oregano, crumbled

1 clove garlic, minced
1/4 tsp. dried dillweed
Grated Parmesan cheese (optional)

Cut bread diagonally into 1" slices. Spread butter and herb mixture on both sides of each slice. Sprinkle liberally with Parmesan cheese. Heat in hot 400° oven for 10 to 15 minutes.

ORANGE MARMALADE BREAD

3 C. all-purpose flour
3 tsp. baking powder
1 egg, well beaten
1/4 C. sugar

Pinch salt
1/2 C. orange marmalade
1 C. milk
1/2 C. walnuts, cut up

Mix well. Let stand for 10 minutes. Bake in greased loaf pan for 1 to 1¼ hours at 350°. This may appear hard when taken from the oven. Let it stand overnight to soften.

CHILI PEPPER CORNBREAD

1 1/2 C. cornmeal
1 T. sugar
1/2 tsp. salt*
1/2 tsp. soda*
1 C. milk or buttermilk
2 eggs

1/3 C. oil
1 chopped onion
1 C. grated sharp cheese
1 sm. can cream-style corn
1 sm. can green chili peppers, drained

*If you use self-rising cornmeal, omit salt and soda.

Combine dry ingredients. Combine milk, eggs, and oil, and add to dry ingredients. Add onions, cheese, corn and peppers; mix all ingredients and pour into greased pan. Bake at 425° for 25 minutes or until lightly browned. This is especially good with chili, vegetable soup and beef stew. Serves 6 to 8.

CINNAMON MUFFINS

1 C. flour
1 1/2 tsp. baking powder
1 egg
1/2 C. milk
1/4 C. melted or soft shortening

1 1/2 tsp. cinnamon
1/4 tsp. salt
1/2 C. brown sugar, packed
1/2 C. raisins

Sift flour and baking powder into bowl. Set aside. Blend egg, milk, shortening, cinnamon, salt and brown sugar in blender until smooth. Add raisins. Blend a few seconds and pour over dry ingredients. Stir lightly and turn into greased muffin pans. Bake for 15 to 20 minutes at 375°. Serves 6 to 8.

CRANBERRY ORANGE MUFFINS

2 C. flour
3 tsp. baking powder
1 egg
1 C. milk
1 C. cranberries

Rind of 2 oranges
3 T. soft or melted shortening (Crisco)
2/3 C. sugar
1 tsp. salt

Sift flour and baking powder into a bowl. Set aside. Place all remaining ingredients in blender and blend until cranberries are chopped fine. Pour over dry ingredients and stir just to moisten flour. Spoon into greased muffin pans and bake in 400° oven for 25 minutes. Makes 1 1/2 dozen.

TOADS

2 cans refrigerated biscuits
Oil, to fry

1 1/2 C. powdered sugar, sifted

Heat 2 1/2" of oil in a heavy skillet. Open cans of biscuits and drop, one-by-one, in hot oil. When brown on one side, turn and brown other side. Drain on paper towels. Roll in sifted powdered sugar. Serve hot or warm.

Note: Biscuits will puff up when fried.

- SIDE DISHES -

BUTTER-SIMMERED CARROTS

4 C. raw carrots
1 T. butter

2 to 3 T. sugar
1 tsp. salt

Wash, scrape and slice carrots lengthwise. Put into heavy saucepan with butter, sugar and salt. Cover closely and simmer until tender. Makes 8 to 10 servings.

OKRA SLIME

1 lb. okra
2 C. boiling water

1 tsp. salt
2 T. butter

Wash okra; cut off stem ends. If pods are large, cut in 1/2" pieces; if small, leave whole. Cook uncovered in boiling, salted water to cover for 5 minutes; cover the pan, cook about 5 minutes or until tender. Drain, season, add butter and serve with rice.

FRIED ONION RING HAYSTACKS

1 lg. Bermuda onion
1 C. flour
1 1/2 tsp. baking powder
1/2 tsp. salt

1 egg
2/3 C. water
1 tsp. lemon juice
1 tsp. melted shortening

Slice onion and separate rings carefully. Mix remaining ingredients until just blended. Coat onion rings in batter and deep fry until brown and crisp. Drain. Stack in a mound like a haystack to serve.

Strain and refrigerate cooking oil. To re-use, add half new oil to old.

. . . hearts go home for the holidays

ONIONS AND APPLES

1/4 C. shortening or bacon drippings
4 C. onions, sliced
4 C. apples, quartered

2 tsp. salt
2 T. sugar

Heat shortening in a skillet; add onions and apples. Cover and steam 10 minutes, stirring occasionally until apples are soft and onions tender and slightly browned. Add salt and sugar. Serve hot.

PINEAPPLE CASSEROLE

1 20-oz. can pineapple chunks
   (do not drain)
3 eggs, beaten until frothy
1/2 C. granulated sugar
2 T. plain flour

1/2 tsp. salt
4 slices white bread, crusts removed,
   bread cut into cubes
2/3 stick butter or margarine, melted

In a large mixing bowl, combine pineapple juice and beaten eggs. In a separate bowl, sift together sugar, flour and salt. Add to pineapple mixture. Pour into a buttered 9x9" casserole dish. Toss bread cubes in melted butter. Place on top of casserole. Bake at 350° for 35 to 45 minutes or until bread cubes are lightly brown. Do not overcook. Serve hot.

POTATOES ANNA

4 lg. raw potatoes
1/4 lb. butter

Salt and pepper
Paprika

Pare potatoes, cut in 1/8" slices crosswise. Drop into cold water. Drain and dry. Dip each slice into melted butter and line a buttered, heavy skillet with overlapping slices. There should be no more than 3 layers. Season well and dot with butter. Place in very hot 450° oven for 10 minutes; reduce heat to 350° and bake until tender and browned, about 30 minutes longer. Invert on platter.

Note: For easier clean up and serving, line skillet with heavy foil before layering potatoes.

Cook a very large pot of rice. Cool and place in several Ziploc bags in the amount you'll need per meal. Freeze. When ready to use, microwave until hot. This will keep up to 3 months in your freezer. Convenient and no pot to wash!

Whenever possible, cook potatoes in their skins to retain nutrients, then peel and use according to recipe.

Chop several large onions. Freeze in Ziploc bags. Ready when you need them.

- MAIN DISHES -

JACK-O'-LANTERN SANDWICHES

8 pieces whole-wheat bread (or brown bread such as pumpernickel or rye)   **4 American cheese slices (thick style)**

Cut 4 slices of bread to look like jack-o'-lantern faces. Cut out 2 small triangles for eyes, 1 for the nose and a large inverted triangle for the mouth. These will be the tops of sandwiches. Spread 4 bottom slices of bread with small amount of mayonnaise. Place 1 thick slice of cheese on each and top with the cut out top slice of bread. The cheese shows through like a jack-o'-lantern's face.

Place sandwiches in a toaster oven and toast until lightly brown and cheese is softened. Makes 4 servings.

Even spookier when the cheese "oozes" out around the edges!

DIRTY RICE

1 lb. ground or finely chopped chicken livers
1 C. finely chopped onion
1/2 C. chopped celery
1 bunch green onions, chopped, with tops

1 clove garlic
1 pod red pepper
2 qt. boiler cooked rice (almost done)
2 C. water
Salt, to taste

Finely chop liver, onions, celery and garlic. Add water and red pepper. Cook for 7 to 8 minutes, stirring. Mix rice and liver well and pour into buttered 9x13" casserole dish. Bake at 350° for 15 minutes. Serve hot.

GLORIFIED FRIED CHICKEN

1 (2 1/2-lb.) frying chicken   **2 tsp. Accent**

Cut chicken into serving pieces. Sprinkle with Accent; set aside while preparing Marinade.

Marinade:
1 C. sour cream
2 cloves garlic, crushed

1 T. lemon juice
1 tsp. Worcestershire sauce

Blend all ingredients in a medium bowl. Dip chicken in Marinade to coat each piece. Cover bowl and refrigerate overnight. Dredge sour cream chicken pieces in dry bread crumbs to which 1 1/2 teaspoons Seasoned Salt has been added. Fry in 1 cup cooking oil until browned and crisp on both sides. Reduce heat and fry slowly until tender (about 45 minutes). Do not crowd in pan. Cover for first 20 minutes.

Seasoned Salt:
2 tsp. salt
1/2 tsp. coarse black pepper

1/2 tsp. thyme
1/2 tsp. ginger

Combine ingredients.

FROGMORE STEW

3 T. Old Bay Seasoning or
   homemade boil
3 T. salt
2 gal. water
2 lb. Hillshire Farms hot, smoked link
   sausage, cut into 2" pieces

12 ears yellow corn, freshly shucked,
   broken into 3 to 4" pieces
24 sm. whole new red potatoes
   (do not peel)
4 lb. raw shrimp

In a large stockpot, add seasoning to water; bring to a boil. Add sausage and boil, uncovered, for 5 minutes. Add corn and potatoes and count 5 minutes. Add the shrimp and cook 3 minutes. (Don't wait for the liquid to return to a boil before timing the corn, potatoes and shrimp.) Drain immediately. Place a large bowl in center of table; pour drained food into bowl for everyone to serve themselves. Serve with a green leafy salad or coleslaw.

SIMPLE SHRIMP CREOLE

1/4 C. salad oil
1 C. thinly sliced onion
1 C. thinly sliced celery
1 C. green pepper strips, about 2" long
3 1/2 C. canned tomatoes
1 8-oz. can tomato sauce
2 bay leaves
1 T. salt

1 T. sugar
1 T. chili powder
1/8 tsp. Tabasco sauce
1 lb. cooked, cleaned shrimp
   (3 1/2 to 4 C.)
2 T. flour
1/3 C. water

Heat oil in frying pan; saute onions, celery and green pepper until tender, but not brown -- about 5 minutes. Add tomatoes, tomato sauce, bay leaves, salt, sugar, chili powder, Tabasco sauce and shrimp; mix well; cover. Simmer 30 minutes. Combine flour and water; add to mixture in frying pan and cook until thickened, about 5 minutes. Serve over rice.

SLOPPY JOES

Beef Mixture:
1 lb. ground beef
1/2 C. chopped onion
1 T. olive oil

1/2 tsp. Accent
1/2 tsp. salt
1/8 tsp. pepper

Brown ground beef and onions in olive oil. Add Accent, salt and pepper. Pour Sauce over cooked ground beef. Simmer for 15 minutes. Serve on heated buns. Makes 4 to 5 servings.

Sauce:
1 can tomato soup (do not dilute)
2 T. brown sugar
2 T. lemon juice

1 tsp. prepared mustard
1 tsp. Worcestershire sauce

Combine ingredients in a bowl.
Quick and easy for your own "trick or treaters".

MONSTER MELTS

3 English muffins, split and
   lightly buttered
6 tomato slices

8 slices bacon, fried crisp
   and crumbled
6 slices American cheese

Place buttered muffin halves in broiler for 2 minutes until lightly brown and warm; remove from heat. Place on each muffin half a slice of tomato, crumbled bacon and then a slice of cheese. Return to broiler and broil until cheese is melted, about 1 minute. Yield: 6 servings.

RINKTIN DITY

1 can tomato soup (undiluted)
1 egg, well beaten
1 lb. Cheddar cheese, grated
1 T. Worcestershire sauce

Salt and pepper, to taste
Toast points
6 to 8 slices bacon, fried crisp
   and crumbled

Rinse saucepan with cold water. Heat; add soup and egg. Bring to a slow boil. Add cheese, Worcestershire sauce, salt and pepper. Simmer until cheese melts. Serve on toast points. Garnish with bacon. Serves 6.

- DESSERTS -

EARTHQUAKE CAKE

1 1/2 C. chopped pecans
1 1/2 C. shredded coconut
1 bx. German chocolate cake mix

1/2 C. margarine
1 8-oz. pkg. cream cheese
4 C. powdered sugar

In mixing bowl, prepare cake mix using directions on package. Preheat oven to 350°. Grease and flour a 9x13" pan. Combine pecans and coconut. Sprinkle in bottom of pan. Pour prepared cake mix over top of pecans and coconut. In a saucepan, melt butter and cream cheese together. Add powdered sugar and mix well. Pour over cake batter. Bake at 350° for 45 to 50 minutes. Cool and cut into squares. Makes 6 servings.

Sift together 1 part cornstarch and 3 parts all-purpose flour to make your own cake flour.

To keep fruits and nuts from sinking to the bottom of a cake; first heat them in oven and mix with small amount of flour.

. . . hearts go home for the holidays

ORANGE LAYER CAKE

1 3/4 C. sifted cake flour
1/4 C. butter
1/2 C. sugar
2 eggs, beaten without separating

Grated rind of 1 orange
1/2 C. milk
3 level tsp. baking powder

Bake the cake in 2 or 3 layers; put the layers together with the Filling between the layers and Frosting on top and sides of cake.

Filling:
1 egg or 2 yolks
1 C. sugar

2 T. butter
1 orange, grated rind and juice

Beat the whole egg or the yolks; add the other ingredients and cook over boiling water until the mixture thickens. Use when cold.

Frosting:
1 orange, grated rind and juice
Confectioner's sugar

1 T. lemon juice

Stir the sifted sugar into the liquid to make a mixture stiff enough to remain in place. A beaten yolk of egg may be used to heighten the orange tint.

ORANGE POUND CAKE

1 tsp. salt
1 3/4 C. flour
2 tsp. baking powder
1/4 C. sugar
1/2 C. vegetable oil

1 tsp. orange rind
1/2 C. orange juice
4 eggs
1 tsp. orange extract (optional)

Sift salt, flour and baking powder together in a mixing bowl. Mix with sugar until well blended. Gradually add oil, orange juice, orange rind and eggs and mix with electric mixer at least 3 minutes. Pour into greased and floured loaf pan. Bake at 350° for 45 minutes.

Glaze:
1 C. confectioner's sugar
1 T. orange juice

1 tsp. grated orange rind

Combine ingredients.

ORANGE CREAM CHEESE FROSTING

Blend 2 tablespoons butter or margarine with 2 3-ounce packages cream cheese. Alternately add 4 cups sifted confectioner's sugar and 2 tablespoons frozen orange juice concentrate, beating until smooth.

FOXHEAD PIE

2 eggs, slightly beaten
1 C. sugar
1 stick butter
1 C. chopped pecans

1 C. chocolate chips
1 T. vanilla
1/2 C. flour (add last)

Combine eggs, sugar, melted butter, vanilla, nuts and chocolate chips. Mix; add flour and mix again. Bake in unbaked pie shell for 30 minutes at 350°.

JACK-O'-LANTERN TARTS

Pastry for 2-crust pie
3/4 C. canned pumpkin
1 6-oz. can evaporated milk (undiluted)
1 C. light brown sugar, firmly packed

2 eggs, slightly beaten
2 tsp. pumpkin pie spice
1/2 tsp. salt

Divide pastry into 8 equal portions. On lightly floured surface, roll each portion into a 5" circle. Use to line 8 (3 1/2") tart pans or 8 (5-ounce) custard cups, pressing each circle firmly to bottom and side. Trim pastry from top edge. Re-roll trimmings. Cut into 8 (1 1/2") circles. Then trim each circle to resemble a pumpkin. Refrigerate, on wax paper, along with tart shells until ready to use. Meanwhile, preheat oven to 400°. In large bowl, using rotary beater, beat pumpkin, evaporated milk and sugar. Add remaining ingredients, beating until well combined. Pour pumpkin mixture into each tart shell. Bake tarts, on cookie sheet, 25 to 30 minutes or until knife inserted in filling comes out clean. Last 10 minutes of baking, place a pumpkin cutout on each tart. Let cool on wire rack. Serve garnished with whipped cream, if desired. Yield: 8 servings.

MUD PIE

1 C. chocolate wafer cookie crumbs
1/4 C. (1/2 stick) unsalted butter,
   melted
1 qt. coffee ice cream, softened

1 1/4 C. purchased fudge sauce
Chopped, toasted almonds
1 C. chilled whipping cream

The day before serving, mix chocolate cookie crumbs and melted butter in bowl until crumbs are moistened. Press onto bottom and up sides of 9" glass pie dish. Freeze crust 10 minutes. Spread softened ice cream evenly in crust. Freeze 20 minutes. Pour fudge sauce over ice cream. (If fudge sauce is too thick to pour or spread, heat over low heat until just pourable.) Freeze pie overnight. Sprinkle nuts over pie. Beat cream to stiff peaks. Spoon into pastry bag fitted with medium star tip. Pipe cream decoratively atop pie. Cut into wedges.

TAFFY PIE IN GINGERSNAP CRUST

2 eggs
2 tsp. water
1 T. melted butter

2 tsp. vanilla
1 1/2 C. dark brown sugar
1 C. pecans

Place eggs, water, melted butter, vanilla and brown sugar in blender and blend a few seconds to mix well. Add pecans and blend until chopped. Pour into Gingersnap Pie Crust.

Gingersnap Pie Crust:
1 1/4 C. blender-crushed gingersnaps   1 T. sugar
1/3 C. melted butter

Combine crumbs, butter and sugar and pack firmly over bottom and sides of 9" pie pan. Keep out a few crumbs to sprinkle over the top of the pie if you like. Chill this crust. Don't bake it. If you like, use crumbs just for the bottom of the pie and stand whole cookies up around the rim.

HAYSTACKS

1 12-oz. pkg. butterscotch morsels
2 T. peanut butter

4 to 5 oz. Spanish peanuts
1 lg. can Chinese noodles

Melt morsels and peanut butter in double boiler. Pour in noodles and peanuts; stir until coated. Drop by spoonfuls onto wax paper. Store in airtight container.

TRICKY TREATS

2 egg whites, beaten
1/8 tsp. cream of tartar

1/2 C. granulated sugar
3/4 C. M&M's (assorted colors)

Preheat oven to 250°. In a small bowl, combine egg whites and cream of tartar; beat until stiff peaks form. Add sugar, 1 tablespoon at a time. Fold M&M's into egg whites. Drop by teaspoonfuls onto a greased and floured cookie sheet. Bake for 30 minutes. Cool slightly, then remove and cool completely on wire rack. Makes 2 dozen.

When making fruit pies, mix 2 tablespoons flour and 2 tablespoons sugar. Spread over unbaked crust, then add fruit filling.

Chill flour and shortening for pie crust 1 hour before mixing. Makes a very flaky crust.

FROST ON THE PUMPKIN COOKIES

1 C. sifted all-purpose flour
2 tsp. baking powder
1 tsp. cinnamon
1/4 tsp. nutmeg
1/4 tsp. ginger
1/4 tsp. salt
1/4 C. soft butter or margarine

1/2 C. light brown sugar, firmly packed
1/2 C. canned pumpkin
1 egg
1/2 C. chopped almonds
1/4 C. diced candied orange peel
1/4 C. light raisins

Preheat oven to 350°. Sift flour with baking powder, cinnamon, nutmeg, ginger and salt; set aside. In large bowl of electric mixer, at medium speed, beat butter with sugar until light and fluffy. Beat in pumpkin and egg. Stir in flour mixture, almonds, orange peel and raisins; mix well. Drop cookie dough by rounded teaspoonfuls, 2" apart, onto lightly greased cookie sheets. Flatten slightly. Bake for 20 minutes or until firm. Remove to wire rack; let cool completely. Makes about 2 1/2 dozen.

Frost with 2 cups sifted confectioner's sugar mixed with 2 to 3 tablespoons lemon juice or milk until smooth. Add more liquid if needed.

ORANGE SPICE BARS

1 6-oz. can frozen orange juice
  concentrate, thawed
1/2 C. quick-cooking rolled oats
1/2 C. mixed candied fruits and peels
1/2 C. chopped walnuts
1 3/4 C. all-purpose flour
1 tsp. baking soda

1 tsp. ground ginger
1 tsp. ground cinnamon
1/2 C. shortening
1/2 C. sugar
1/2 C. molasses
1 egg
Orange Icing

Combine concentrate, oats, fruits, and nuts; set aside. Combine flour, soda, spices, and 1/4 teaspoon salt; set aside. Cream shortening and sugar until fluffy. Beat in molasses and egg. Add flour mixture and fruit mixture alternately to creamed mixture, beating well after each addition. Turn into a greased 13x9" baking pan. Bake in 325° oven for 35 to 40 minutes. Cool on wire rack; frost with Orange Icing. Makes 3 dozen.

Orange Icing:
    Blend 1 1/2 cups sifted powdered sugar with 4 to 6 teaspoons orange juice.

PEANUT BUTTER CHOCOLATE BARS

1/2 C. margarine
1 1/2 C. graham cracker crumbs
1 can sweetened condensed milk

1 12-oz. pkg. semi-sweet
  chocolate chips
1 C. peanut butter chips

Place a 13x9" glass baking dish in a preheated 350° oven. Put margarine in dish and melt in oven. Distribute crumbs evenly over melted margarine. Pour milk evenly over crumbs. Combine chocolate and peanut butter chips in a bowl and place on top of milk. Press the chips down into the milk and crumbs. Bake in a preheated oven at 325° for 25 to 30 minutes until slightly browned. Remove from oven. Cool and cut into bars. Makes 3 dozen.

S'MORES

12 graham crackers   24 lg. toasted marshmallows
6 plain chocolate bars, cut in fourths

Break graham crackers into 2 squares. Place 1/4 of chocolate bar on each square. Toast a large marshmallow. Place on chocolate candy, immediately top with another graham cracker square.

Wonderful! You'll want some more!

Note: Perfect dessert for an autumn weiner roast -- the coals will be just right for toasting the marshmallows.

WITCH'S HATS

1 1-oz. square unsweetened chocolate   3 C. Puffed Wheat or
16 soft marshmallows   Rice Krispie cereal
3 T. Karo corn syrup

Cut eight 3 1/2" paper circles from black construction paper. Place cereal in shallow pan in oven at 350° for 10 minutes. Meanwhile, in a saucepan, melt chocolate, marshmallows, and corn syrup. Stir until blended. Pour heated cereal into a greased bowl. Pour chocolate mixture over cereal. Stir to coat evenly. Grease your hands and form mixture into 8 little cone shapes. Place large end down on 8 paper circles (for hat brims).

Note: These can be used as edible placecards if you like. Just write the names on hat brims in white ink or white chalk.

Egg whites will whip easier and lightly if they are at room temperature.

Grated lemon or orange rind/zest freezes well. Keep small amounts on hand for recipes requiring them.

Put bowl and beaters in freezer for 30 minutes before using to whip cream.

Add a pinch of baking soda to whipping cream to make it whip quicker and lighter.

. . . hearts go home for the holidays

Thanksgiving

- PARTY FOODS -

PASTRY CORNUCOPIA

4 C. all-purpose flour	Aluminum foil
2 tsp. salt	1 egg, beaten
1 1/2 C. shortening	2 tsp. cold water
2 eggs, beaten	* * *
1/3 C. water	1 or 2 T. milk
* * *	Sugar

Combine flour and salt in a large bowl; mix well. Cut in shortening. Beat 2 eggs with 1/3 cup cold water. Stir into flour mixture with a fork until flour is moistened. Add a little more water if necessary. With fingers, gather dough into a ball; divide into 4 equal pieces. Wrap each in plastic wrap and refrigerate until ready to use.

Crumple 12 large pieces of aluminum foil into balls to make shape of cornucopia. Place each foil ball in center of a 20" sheet of foil. Bring ends up over balls and fold. Using your hands, shape the foil into a cornucopia with open end being about 5" high and the cornucopia 10 to 12" long.

Take one of the pieces of dough and roll it on a floured cloth-covered surface into a triangle shape about 1 1/2" longer than base of cornucopia mold. Place mold on pastry base -- open end to the large end if triangle, tip end at the small end of pastry base. Lift pastry base and mold together onto ungreased cookie sheet.

Take the second piece of pastry and roll into a 15x10" oval. Cut into 1" strips lengthwise (a pastry cutter or pizza cutter works just fine for this).

Mix egg with 2 teaspoons cold water. Brush one short strip with egg mixture and place egg mixture side out around tip of mold to form a point. Continue brushing egg mixture on one strip at a time (starting with shorter strips) and drape over mold (egg mixture side out) with strips overlapping 1/4". Let excess of strips lie on pastry base.

Take third piece of pastry dough out and roll into a 15x10" oval. Continue to add strips until mold is covered (do not cover opening). Press gently where strips are overlapped to be sure that there are no gaps.

Divide remaining piece of pastry into thirds. Take first one-third and roll it into a rope 24" long and 1/4" thick. Flatten with rolling pin to 1/2" wide. Cut strip in half lengthwise and twist two pieces together loosely. Place around opening and press ends together. Brush with egg mixture. Cut excess dough from form. Place twisted dough around base. Cut any remaining pieces of dough into shapes . . . grapes, leaves, etc. Attach using egg mixture brushed under and over shapes. Then brush entire cornucopia with egg mixture. Heat oven to 425°. Bake for 10 minutes and remove from oven.

Brush with milk; generously sprinkle with sugar. Reduce oven to 350°. Return cornucopia on cookie sheet back into the oven and bake 10 to 25 minutes longer. If it browns too quickly, you may want to cover tip and edges of opening with a strip of foil. Cool on cookie sheet for 5 minutes. Lift carefully with large spatula onto a wire rack to cool. Cool 40 to 50 minutes.

Remove foil carefully and you'll have a masterpiece of a cornucopia. Fill with rolls or cookies and use for a centerpiece. Store, covered loosely, in a cool, dry place. Do not refrigerate after baking.

Note: Frozen pastry may be used for this. You will need two 17-ounce packages.

The unbaked cornucopia can be molded and brushed with egg mixture and refrigerated 24 hours (wrapped carefully) or may be frozen for up to 1 month.

Variation: Pastry dough may be used to wrap fully cooked canned hams. Use your imagination and cut decorative shapes for tops of ham. Use egg mixture and a milk and sugar glaze.

AUTUMN APRICOT BALLS

1/2 C. light corn syrup
2 T. butter, softened
1 T. water
1/2 tsp. vanilla extract

2/3 C. dry non-fat powdered milk
2 C. finely chopped dried apricots
2 C. shredded coconut
Confectioner's sugar

Mix syrup and butter until smooth. Add water, vanilla and powdered milk. Mix apricots and coconut together. Add to mixture and knead with hands until ingredients are blended. Shape into 3/4" balls. Roll in sifted confectioner's sugar. Keep in tins.
These are easy and tasty!

HOLIDAY COOKIE CUTTER SANDWICHES

1 3-oz. pkg. soft cream cheese
1/3 C. orange marmalade
8 white bread slices

8 whole-wheat bread slices
1/4 C. soft butter or margarine

In small bowl, combine cheese with marmalade, mixing until well combined. With sharp knife or scissors, trim crusts from bread. With appropriate holiday shape cookie cutter, cut out center of 4 white bread slices and 4 whole-wheat bread slices. Set cutouts and cutout bread slices aside. Spread with butter; then spread with cream cheese mixture. Serve open face.

HOT 'N SPICY CHEESE PUFFS

2 C. biscuit baking mix
6 T. butter or margarine,
    room temperature
6 T. chopped green chili peppers

2 eggs, beaten
2 C. grated sharp Cheddar cheese
2 tsp. dried cilantro

Combine baking mix, butter, chili peppers and eggs. Mix well. Fold in cheese and cilantro. Place on a greased cookie sheet about 1 1/2" apart. Bake at 400° in a preheated oven for 12 minutes or until lightly browned. Store in an airtight container.

NUT CHEESE WAFERS

1 stick butter or margarine, softened
1 C. plain flour
1 tsp. cayenne pepper

2 C. grated sharp Cheddar cheese
1 C. finely chopped pecans
1/4 tsp. salt

In a mixing bowl, combine all ingredients. Mix well. Shape into 2 rolls about 1 1/2" in diameter. Wrap in plastic wrap and refrigerate 8 to 10 hours. Slice into thin wafers and bake in a preheated 375° oven for 8 to 10 minutes. Check them often as they burn easily.
Note: May be frozen and then sliced when needed.

VEGETABLE CENTERPIECE

1 18" styrofoam cone or wooden cone
   with finishing nails
2 bunches fresh spinach
2 bunches fresh parsley

Fresh whole vegetables*
Persimmons
Nuts

*Use radishes, carrots, small eggplants, potatoes, sweet potatoes, green and red pepper, bunches of green beans, large fresh mushrooms, broccoli, squash and cauliflower, just to mention a few.

Cover cone with spinach leaves attached by toothpicks or florist pins. Attach vegetables with large toothpicks in any pattern you desire (use your imagination). Surround base with spinach leaves and parsley.

You may create special affect by separating cauliflower into flowerets and chilling them in water. Cut celery into 1 1/2" lengths and make several slits half the length of the celery stick and chill in water until the ends curl. To make carrot daisies, pare carrot and cut into 3 pieces. Cut 5 to 6 lengthwise notches around the carrot and slice into 1/2" rounds. Place green pepper square atop carrot slices and attach with toothpicks. Use your imagination with other vegetables.

Note: This makes a beautiful centerpiece! Take it apart and make a pot of soup using the vegetables and any leftover meat you might have in the refrigerator.

DRIED FRUIT AND DIP

1 pkg. assorted dried fruits

1 bot. Knott's Berry Farm
   fruit salad dressing

This is so easy it's almost embarrassing!

Open the bag of fruit. Arrange it in a single layer on a tray. Pour the bottle of dressing into a small dish. It's ready! Just dip and eat.

Good and good for you.

RAW VEGETABLE DIP

1 C. mayonnaise
1 tsp. vinegar
1 tsp. grated horseradish

1 tsp. grated onion
1/2 to 1 tsp. curry powder

Mix ingredients well and chill before serving. Serve with assorted raw vegetables.

For perfect boiled eggs, bring eggs to boil. Cover and remove from heat. Let stand covered for 15 minutes.

CHEESE "CORN-ON-THE-COB" SPREAD

1 lg. ear corn, in a fresh green husk
1 8-oz. pkg. cream cheese, softened
1 8-oz. pkg. Cheddar cheese, shredded

Dash turmeric, for color
1 tsp. hickory smoked salt (Durkees)

Cream cheeses together. Add seasonings; set aside. Carefully remove husk from corn keeping husk as intact as possible. Peel back just enough of the husk in order to cut the ear of corn from it leaving the stem end together with husk still attached. Remove any silks. Rinse whole husks in cold water and pat dry inside and out. Shape the cheese mixture into the shape of an ear of corn (use the one you removed as a model). Using a knife, make lines in the cheese to resemble corn kernels. You can make it look as real as you like. Place the "cheese" ear of corn back in the husk as if it were the real one. Peel back enough of the husk to enable slicing of the cheese. Serve with crackers.

TURKEY SPREAD

1/4 C. sherry
1 16-oz. ctn. cottage cheese
1/4 C. Hellmann's mayonnaise
1/2 tsp. seasoned salt

1/8 tsp. black pepper
2 C. cooked turkey, cubed
2 T. chopped chives

Mix all ingredients in food processor or blender until smooth. May be used as spread for toast points or crackers or as a dip. Garnish with additional chives.
Great dish for leftover turkey!

- BEVERAGES -

AUTUMN GLOW PUNCH

1 orange
About 12 whole cloves
2 bot. (4/5-qt. size) claret
1 lemon, sliced
1 (1 1/2") cinnamon stick

1/2 C. blanched whole almonds
1/2 C. dark raisins
1/2 C. sugar
1/2 C. cognac or brandy

Preheat oven to 400°. Wash orange; with sharp knife, score skin into diamond pattern. Stud each diamond with a clove. Place in shallow baking pan; bake, uncovered, for 30 minutes. Meanwhile, in large saucepan, combine claret, lemon slices, cinnamon stick, almonds, raisins and 1/4 cup sugar. Add baked orange; over low heat, bring to simmering. Simmer, uncovered, 15 to 20 minutes, stirring occasionally. Remove cinnamon stick. Pour punch into punch bowl. Combine rest of sugar and the cognac in small saucepan; heat very gently.
Light with match. While it is flaming, pour into punch bowl. Serve hot after flame goes out.
This is a "grown-up's" punch. Handle carefully.

AUTUMN HARVEST PUNCH

2 C. water
2 C. sugar
4 cinnamon sticks
36 whole cloves
2 qt. cranberry juice
1 qt. orange juice

2 C. bot. lemon juice
1 lemon, sliced
1 orange, sliced
1 C. rum (optional) or
  2 T. rum flavoring

In a large pot, bring water, cinnamon sticks and cloves to a boil. Reduce heat to low and simmer for 5 to 7 minutes. Remove cinnamon sticks and cloves; pour in remaining ingredients and heat. Serve hot. Garnish with lemon and orange slices. Makes 24 servings.

Smells heavenly! Tastes great! Beautiful amber color.

Serving suggestion: Serve from a glass punch bowl surrounded by autumn leaves, nuts, fruits, Indian corn.

HOLIDAY PUNCH

3 cans frozen orange juice
3 cans frozen lemonade
1 can pineapple juice

14 C. cold water
1 bot. ginger ale, chilled
Thin slices of oranges, for garnish

Mix first 4 ingredients. Chill. When ready to serve, add ginger ale. Garnish with orange slices. Makes 50 servings.

- SOUPS -

BARLEY VEGETABLE SOUP

2 lb. soup bone with meat
  (ham or beef)
2 T. shortening
8 C. water
1 1/2 tsp. salt
1/4 tsp. pepper
1/4 C. barley
1 C. cubed potatoes

1 C. cubed carrots
1 can whole kernel corn
1 med. onion, chopped
1/2 C. chopped celery
1 #2 can green lima beans
2 C. canned tomatoes
1 #2 can cut green beans

Cook soup bone. Remove meat; cut into cubes and brown in shortening. Place bone, meat cubes, water, salt and pepper in large pot; cover and simmer for 1 hour. Add barley; cook 1 more hour. Cool and remove bone. Add remaining ingredients; cook until carrots are tender. Yield: 10 servings.

CONSOMME PRINCESS

2 cans beef consomme
1 sm. can LeSueur English peas,
   drained
Cold cooked chicken breasts,
   cut into tiny cubes

1 doz. saltine crackers
Butter
A few grains of cayenne

Heat consomme to boiling point. Add drained peas and cubes of chicken breasts. Reheat. Serve with browned crackers. Spread saltines with butter; sprinkle with a few grains of cayenne. Brown delicately in a 375° oven, being careful not to burn. Serve at once.

Note: Browned crackers are good with any soup, anytime.

OYSTER STEW

1 pt. oysters with liquid
2 C. milk
2 C. Half and Half
1/4 C. butter or margarine
1 tsp. salt

1/4 tsp. white or black pepper
Dash cayenne
Dash mace
1 T. dried chives or 2 T. fresh, minced
Oyster crackers

Drain liquid from oysters into a saucepan. Set oysters aside. Turn heat on medium. Add milk, Half and Half, butter, salt, pepper, cayenne, mace and chives. Heat to boiling point. Add oysters and simmer just until edges curl. Serve in heated soup bowls with heated oyster crackers. Makes 8 servings.

Note: Oyster crackers are even better when they have been heated. The stew will not cool as quickly when they're added.

- SALADS -

ALMOND SALAD

3 T. butter or margarine
3/4 C. slivered toasted almonds
2 T. lemon juice
1/4 C. salad oil

1/4 tsp. salt
2 tsp. sugar
1 head crisp Boston lettuce, broken
   into bite-size pieces

Melt butter in small skillet. Add almonds, and saute over low heat until lightly browned, 3 to 4 minutes. Drain on paper towels. In jar with tight-fitting lid, combine lemon juice, salad oil, salt, and sugar; shake until well combined. In salad bowl, toss dressing with lettuce and almonds, coating lettuce well. Makes 4 servings.

AUTUMN HARVEST SALAD

2 env. unflavored gelatin
1/4 C. sugar
1/2 tsp. salt
1 chicken bouillon cube dissolved
   in 1 1/2 C. boiling water
1/3 C. tarragon-wine vinegar

1/2 C. lemon juice
1 10-oz. pkg. frozen peas and carrots
1 C. canned whole kernel corn, drained
1 C. finely shredded green cabbage
Salad greens

In large bowl, combine gelatin with sugar and salt; add hot bouillon, stirring until gelatin is dissolved. Stir in vinegar, lemon juice, and 1 1/4 cups cold water. Refrigerate until consistency of unbeaten egg white, about 1½ to 2 hours. Meanwhile, cook peas and carrots as package label directs; drain and refrigerate until ready to use. Gently fold vegetables into gelatin mixture. Turn into a 1½-quart mold or into a 9x5x3" loaf pan. Refrigerate until firm, 3 to 4 hours. To unmold, run a small spatula around edge of mold. Invert over platter; shake gently to release. If necessary, place a hot, damp dish cloth over bottom of mold; shake again to release. Garnish with salad greens. Makes 4 to 6 servings.

CARROT, RAISIN, PINEAPPLE SALAD

2/3 C. raisins, washed and drained
2 C. carrots, shredded
1 C. crushed pineapple, drained
1/3 C. Hellmann's mayonnaise

1 T. lemon juice
1/4 tsp. salt
1 T. sugar

Mix raisins, carrots and pineapple together. Set aside. Stir together remaining ingredients. Add to raisin mixture. Chill. Serve on lettuce leaves.

CRANBERRY SALAD
Betty Wilkins - Prosperity, SC

1 pkg. fresh cranberries
1 orange
1 C. chopped nuts
1 6-oz. pkg. black cherry gelatin

2 C. sugar
1 9-oz. can crushed pineapple
   (do not drain)

Put cranberries, orange and nuts in food processor. Process until orange is in small bits. Drain and reserve juices. Dissolve gelatin in 2 1/2 cups hot water. Add sugar; stir until dissolved. Add reserved juices. Chill until partially congealed. Stir in pineapple, cranberries, orange and nuts. Chill until firm. Cut in squares. Serve on lettuce leaves. Top with Hellmann's mayonnaise or whipped cream. Makes 8 to 10 servings.

Try grating broccoli stems for slaw instead of or with cabbage.

Cut an X not quite all the way to the bottom of a cocktail tomato. Insert sprig of parsley in X. Makes a nice garnish and is pretty in individual tossed salads.

To make celery crisp, cut a medium-size potato in 6 pieces. Drop in container with celery, cover with water. Refrigerate. Crisps even old celery.

CRANBERRY VELVET SALAD

16 lg. soft marshmallows
1 C. whipping cream
1 9-oz. can crushed
    pineapple and juice

Pinch of salt
2 T. lemon juice
1/2 tsp. lemon zest (optional)
1 16-oz. can cranberry sauce, drained

In a food processor or blender, combine first 6 ingredients until blended. Then add cranberry sauce. Blend again. Pour into a 9x9" container and freeze at least 3 hours. Cut in squares. Serve on lettuce leaves. Garnish with a sprig of mint. Makes 6 servings.

ENGLISH PEA SALAD

2 cans LeSueur English peas
1 C. finely chopped celery
1 C. finely minced onion or
    thinly sliced green onions

1 C. coarsely chopped nuts
    (peanuts are very good)
2 T. sweet pickle relish
3/4 C. Hellmann's mayonnaise
Paprika, for garnish

Combine all ingredients in a large bowl. Cover and chill. Garnish with paprika when ready to serve. May be made the day before serving. Serves 6 to 8.

STUFFED PRUNE SALAD

12 cooked, pitted prunes, chilled
1/2 C. soft cream cheese
1 tsp. grated orange rind

2 T. chopped nuts
Pinch of salt

Mix cream cheese, orange rind, nuts and salt. Serve on a bed of lettuce or any salad green. Makes 4 servings.

- BREADS -

BROWN BREAD

2 C. All-Bran cereal
2 C. sour milk
2 tsp. pure molasses
1 C. granulated sugar

2 C. all-purpose flour
2 tsp. soda
1 tsp. salt

Mix All-Bran with milk, molasses and sugar. Sift together flour, soda and salt. Add to first mixture. Mix well. Pour into greased loaf pan and bake at 375° for 1 hour. Slice and serve with butter or margarine or spread with your favorite marmalade.
    Delicious and so good for you too!

PUMPKIN BREAD

1/2 C. slivered almonds, chopped
2 tsp. margarine
1 C. sugar
1 egg
1 16-oz. can pumpkin

3 C. biscuit baking mix
1 tsp. cinnamon
1/2 tsp. cloves
1/2 tsp. nutmeg
1/2 tsp. ginger

Saute almonds in margarine; cool on paper towels. Combine sugar, egg and pumpkin. Add biscuit mix, spices and toasted almonds. Turn into buttered 9x5" loaf pan. Sprinkle with additional almonds, if desired. Bake at 350° for 50 to 60 minutes. Cool in pan for 10 minutes. Yield: 1 loaf.

RAISIN NUT BREAD

3 C. plain flour
1 C. nuts, chopped
1 1/2 C. milk
Pinch of salt

1 C. golden raisins
1 egg, beaten
3 tsp. baking powder
3/4 C. granulated sugar

Combine ingredients. Bake in a 9x5" greased and floured loaf pan for 45 minutes at 225°. Slice and serve hot or cold.

CORNSTICKS

2 C. yellow cornmeal
1 C. all-purpose flour
1/4 C. sugar
1 T. baking powder
1 tsp. salt

1/2 tsp. baking soda
2 eggs, lightly beaten
2 C. buttermilk
6 T. butter, melted

Preheat oven to hot 425°. Lightly grease cornstick pan. Place in oven to warm while preparing batter. Combine cornmeal, flour, sugar, baking powder, salt and baking soda in large bowl. Add eggs, buttermilk and butter; stir just to moisten. Pour batter into each cornstick mold, filling each about 3/4 full. Bake in preheated oven for about 15 minutes or until tops are lightly browned. Cool in pan on wire rack for 10 minutes.

If you drop and break an egg on the floor or counter, a quick clean up trick is to pour a tablespoon of salt on the egg. It will wipe right up.

NANNIE'S CORNBREAD DRESSING
Sylvia Herring McCurry - Lincolnton, GA
(Wife of Don McCurry - One of the Twelve)

2 C. self-rising flour
1 C. self-rising meal
2 C. buttermilk
3 eggs, beaten
1 stick melted margarine

1 C. celery, chopped
1 or 2 onions, chopped
1 whole cayenne pepper, chopped
2 to 3 C. chicken broth

Combine flour, meal, buttermilk, eggs and margarine. Pour in a greased, heated pan and bake at 400° for 20 to 25 minutes or until lightly browned. When done, turn out into bowl and crumble in pieces. Mix in celery, onions and pepper. Add broth, a little at a time, until mixture is soupy and thick. Pour into a large, greased baking pan. Bake at 350° until brown on top and around edges. Cool slightly. Serves 6 to 8 heartily.

FRUIT & CARROT MUFFINS

1 1/2 C. all-purpose flour
1 tsp. baking powder
1/2 tsp. baking soda
2 tsp. salt
1 8-oz. can crushed pineapple
2 bananas, mashed

3 T. apple juice
1 egg, beaten
1/4 C. oil
1 tsp. vanilla
1 C. shredded carrots

Sift first 4 ingredients together into a large bowl. In another bowl, mix remaining ingredients omitting carrots. Combine with flour mixture. Stir in carrots. Mix gently. Pour into greased muffin tins and bake at 350° for 35 minutes. Makes 12 to 18 muffins.

Note: These may be made in cupcake paper liners in muffin tins or in miniature muffin tins.

ORENA'S BRAN MUFFINS
Orena Cooper - Lincolnton, GA

1 15-oz. bx. Bran Flakes cereal
3 C. granulated sugar
5 C. plain flour
5 tsp. baking soda

1 tsp. salt
4 beaten eggs
1 C. melted shortening or oil
1 qt. buttermilk

Combine ingredients. Mix and store in covered container in refrigerator. To bake, fill greased muffin tins 1/2 full and bake at 400° for 15 to 20 minutes. Makes approximately 8 dozen.

Will keep for 6 weeks in refrigerator.

Note: You may add coconut or cinnamon sugar to vary recipe. Miniature muffins may also be made from this recipe.

FLAVORED BUTTERS

Each makes about 1/2 cup.

Chive Butter:
1 stick butter, softened
1 T. lemon juice

2 T. chopped fresh chives or
green part of scallion

Lime Butter:
1 stick butter, softened
1 T. lime juice

1/2 tsp. grated lime rind

Sweet Red Pepper Butter:
1 stick butter, softened

2 T. bottled roasted red pepper,
finely chopped

Method:
Cut butter into small pieces and place in small mixer bowl. Add other ingredients and beat with mixer or mash with wooden spoon until butter is smooth and all ingredients are well blended. Scrape butter onto a piece of wax paper. Shape into log 6 to 8" long, rolling up paper. Twist ends of paper to seal. Wrap tightly in aluminum foil. Refrigerate for one day for flavors to develop or freeze for longer storage. Slice off pats to spread as desired.

- SIDE DISHES -

BAKED SLICED APPLES

3 green apples
3 red apples
1/2 C. golden raisins
1/2 C. chopped nuts

3/4 C. sugar
1/2 tsp. ground cinnamon
6 tsp. butter (6 pats)

Core apples. Slice in 1/4" thick rounds. Place sliced apples in a buttered baking dish. Top with nuts and raisins. Mix sugar and cinnamon together and sprinkle over top. Place pats of butter over mixture and bake at 350°, covered, until apples are tender. Serve hot with whipped cream or scoop of ice cream.

HOLIDAY BAKED APPLES

6 firm cooking apples
1/2 C. brown sugar
1 T. red cinnamon candies

3 T. butter
3 T. syrup (maple)

Wash the apples and cut in half. Remove cores, but do not peel. Arrange apple halves, cut side up, in a large baking dish. Sprinkle with sugar and candies. Dot with butter and drizzle syrup over top. Bake uncovered at 350° for 30 to 40 minutes. Makes 12 servings.

GOURMET STUFFED PEACHES
Betty Miller Wilkins - Prosperity, SC

1 (1-lb. 14-oz.) can cling peach halves,
   drained
1 (1-lb. 14-oz.) can pineapple slices,
   drained
1 1/2 C. macaroon crumbs
   (almond macaroons)
1/4 C. chopped pecans

1/4 C. melted butter
2 tsp. finely chopped
   candied orange peel
1/2 tsp. powdered allspice
2/3 C. currant jelly
3 T. sherry

Place peach halves on pineapple slices in a shallow baking dish. Combine macaroon crumbs, pecans, butter, orange peel and allspice. Spoon about 2 tablespoons of mixture onto each peach half. Bake in a 350° oven for 15 to 20 minutes. Combine jelly and sherry; heat until jelly is melted. Spoon sauce over hot peaches and pineapple. Makes 8 servings.

SARA'S BAKED CURRIED FRUIT
Sara Winn - Manchester, GA

1/3 C. melted margarine
3/4 C. packed brown sugar
4 1/2 tsp. curry powder
1 can pears, drained

1 can peach halves, drained
1 can pineapple slices
6 red and 6 green cherries

Mix first 3 ingredients in a bowl. Arrange drained fruit in a 9x13" baking dish. Pour margarine mixture over top. Bake at 325° for 1 hour. Serve hot. Makes 8 to 10 servings.
Note: May be baked in hollowed out grapefruit shells. Add the grapefruit sections to the fruit.

CABBAGE SERVING DISH

1 lg. green or red cabbage
   (a pretty one)

A sharp paring knife

Leave outer leaves on and cut slice off bottom of cabbage to make it sit flat. Hollow cabbage out, leaving 1" on sides and bottom. Fill with any cold vegetable, fruit, pasta salad or dip.
Note: Cook the scooped out cabbage or make slaw out of it and put it back in cabbage shell.
Enjoy! You'll get lots of compliments on this.

CORN PUDDING

2 C. fresh corn, cut from cob or
   1 can corn, chopped finely
2 eggs, slightly beaten
1 tsp. salt
1/8 tsp. pepper

1 tsp. sugar
2 T. melted butter or margarine
2 C. milk
1 C. bread crumbs, for topping
   (optional)

Mix well; bake in buttered casserole dish at 350° for 30 minutes. Serves 4 to 6.

. . . hearts go home for the holidays

COUNTRY CREAM-STYLE CORN

6 to 8 ears fresh corn
2 T. butter or bacon drippings
1 tsp. salt
1/2 tsp. pepper

1 pkt. Sweet 'N Low
Water
1 heaping T. flour
3 T. milk

Remove husks and silks from corn. Cut corn off cob (just cut halfway down kernels), then scrape ear in downward motion to remove remaining part of kernels and "milk". Heat butter or drippings in a heavy skillet. Add corn and "milk" from scraping ears. Add 2 to 3 cups water. Reduce heat; stir often. Add water if necessary. Stir in salt, pepper and sweetener. Cook until corn is tender to taste, about 20 minutes. Dissolve flour in milk. Pour a little at a time into corn. Stir to blend until corn thickens. If it becomes too thick, add water and stir.

SUCCOTASH

1 15-oz. can whole kernel corn, drained
1 15-oz. can fancy or small
   lima beans, drained

2 T. butter
1 T. cream
Salt and pepper, to taste

Place butter and cream in a saucepan; add corn and beans. Heat, stir and serve. Makes 6 to 8 servings.
Note: For added color, you may add 1 teaspoon chopped pimiento.

RICE AU GRATIN

1 1/2 C. cooked rice
1 1/2 T. butter or margarine
4 oz. sharp Cheddar cheese, grated
Few grains of cayenne

Milk
1 C. Ritz crackers, crushed fine
2 tsp. melted butter

Butter a 9x9" baking dish. Place a layer of cooked rice on bottom. Dot with butter. Sprinkle with a layer of cheese. Sprinkle a few grains of cayenne over cheese. Repeat layers until all ingredients are used. Pour milk to half the depth of baking dish. Cover with buttered cracker crumbs. Bake at 325° until cheese melts and crumbs are browned. Makes 4 servings.

Squeeze spinach between two dinner plates to drain. Put spinach in one plate, place bottom of second plate on top of spinach. Hold plates together and squeeze and tilt to drain.

To remove onion odor from hands, rub hands with celery.

SQUASH CASSEROLE

2 lb. fresh squash
1 med. onion, chopped
2 T. sugar
1 tsp. salt
2 eggs, beaten
Pepper, to taste

1/2 stick butter
2 T. flour
Milk (enough to make
    thick white sauce)
1 stack Ritz crackers, crushed
1 T. butter

Boil squash and onions until tender. Drain well and mash with a fork until fairly smooth. Add sugar, salt and pepper. Beat eggs. Add to squash mixture; set aside. In a saucepan, combine butter, flour and milk and cook until you have a thick white sauce. Pour into squash; mix well. Pour into a buttered 9x13" baking dish. Top with cracker crumbs. Dot with butter. Bake at 350° for 20 to 25 minutes. Serve hot.

STUFFED SQUASH

6 yellow squash
3 eggs, beaten
3/4 C. sharp Cheddar cheese

3/4 C. saltine or Ritz crackers,
    crumbled finely
Salt and pepper, to taste
Dash paprika, to garnish

Cook whole squash in boiling, salted water until tender, but still firm enough to handle. Drain and cool. Cut squash in half lengthwise. With a teaspoon, scoop out the insides, leaving at least 1/4" on bottom. Combine the scooped out squash with remaining ingredients. Place squash halves in a 9x13" baking dish in 1/3" of water, scooped out side up. Fill with squash mixture. Sprinkle with a little paprika. Bake at 400° for 15 to 18 minutes. Serves 10 to 12.

MAPLE SWEET POTATOES

4 med. sweet potatoes (about 2-lb.)
Boiling water
1 tsp. salt
1 C. maple syrup

3 T. butter or margarine
2 T. milk
1/2 tsp. salt
Dash cinnamon

Scrub potatoes well with vegetable brush. In small amount of boiling, salted (1 teaspoon salt) water in a large saucepan, cook potatoes, covered, 35 minutes or until tender. Drain; peel, and mash with potato masher. Preheat oven to 400°. To mashed potatoes, add maple syrup, butter, milk, 1/2 teaspoon salt, and cinnamon; mix well. Turn into a lightly buttered 1-quart casserole.

. . . hearts go home for the holidays

NANNIE'S CANDIED SWEET POTATOES

M. Maude McCurry - Lincolnton, GA
(Mother of the Twelve)

6 lg. sweet potatoes, peeled and sliced
1 1/2 sticks butter or margarine,
 melted
1 lemon, sliced

1 orange, sliced
2 C. granulated sugar
1/2 C. orange juice
2 tsp. ground cinnamon (optional)

Place potato slices in layers in large buttered casserole dish. Arrange lemon and orange slices on top. Mix sugar and orange juice; pour over other ingredients. Sprinkle on cinnamon. Cover with plastic wrap and let stand for 1 hour. Bake, uncovered, at 350° for 1½ hours. Baste with liquids several times. Serve hot.

Note: 2 teaspoons vanilla extract may be added.

SWEET POTATOES IN ORANGE CUPS

3 lg. oranges
2 16-oz. cans sweet potatoes, drained
1/4 C. butter, melted
1/4 C. brown sugar

1/4 tsp. vanilla
1/4 C. orange juice
Toasted coconut, red cherries and
 fresh mint leaves, for garnish

Cut each orange in half. Squeeze juice into small bowl. Remove pulp from orange halves. Set aside. In mixing bowl, using electric mixer, beat sweet potatoes until smooth. Add butter, brown sugar, vanilla and orange juice. Fill each orange half with mixture. Brush orange half edges with melted butter and bake at 350° for 25 to 30 minutes. Garnish as desired. Makes 6 servings.

HOLLANDAISE SAUCE

1/2 stick butter, melted
2 egg yolks
1 T. lemon juice

1 T. cold water
A few grains of cayenne pepper

Combine all ingredients in double boiler. Cook on low heat; whip with a wire whisk for 3 to 5 minutes.

Delicious sauce for drained asparagus or green beans.

To crisp green vegetables, add 1 tablespoon vinegar to 3 cups cold water; add vegetables and let stand for a while.

- MAIN DISHES -

BAKED PECAN CHICKEN

1 C. biscuit mix or self-rising flour
1 1/2 tsp. salt
2 tsp. paprika
2 T. sesame seed (optional)
1/2 tsp. poultry seasoning (optional)
1/4 to 1/2 C. finely chopped pecans

1 (2 1/2 to 4-lb.) fryer,
   cut into serving pieces
1/2 C. evaporated milk or milk
1/4 to 1/2 C. melted butter or
   margarine

Combine biscuit mix, seasonings and pecans. Dip fryer pieces into evaporated milk; coat with pecan mixture. Place in 13x9x2" baking pan; pour butter over fryer pieces. Bake at 375° for 1 hour or at 300° for 2 hours or until tender. Makes 4 to 6 servings.

"BIRD IN A BAG"

Preheat oven to 350°. Shake 1 tablespoon flour in turkey bag (19x23½") Oven Cooking Bag. Use large size bag (14x20") for 8 to 12-pound turkeys or for turkey breast. Leave flour in bag. Place bag in roasting pan at least 2" deep. The pan should be large enough that the bag does not hang over sides and does not touch oven walls or oven racks. Remove neck and giblets from both cavities of defrosted turkey. Rinse turkey, pat dry and brush with 2 tablespoons vegetable oil. Slice 1 onion and 2 stalks celery and place in bag. Also add to bag 1 quartered apple and 1 halved carrot. Place turkey, breast side up, in bag on top of vegetables. Close bag with nylon tie; cut six 1/2" slits in top of bag. Insert meat thermometer into inner thigh for whole turkey or into thickest part of breast for turkey breast.

Roast until meat thermometer reads 180 to 185° for whole turkey or 170 to 175° for turkey breast.

For easy slicing, let stand in bag 15 minutes after removing from oven. To open, carefully cut or slit top of bag. If bag sticks to turkey, gently loosen bag from turkey before opening bag.

You may also use an ordinary brown paper bag sprayed inside with Pam. Add 1 tablespoon flour.

CREAMED TURKEY IN PATTY SHELLS

2 C. diced, cooked turkey
1/4 C. beef consomme
1 1/2 C. thinly sliced celery
1 C. coarsely chopped, roasted,
   salted almonds
1 C. Hellmann's mayonnaise
2 T. grated onion

2 T. lemon juice
1 pimiento, cut into strips
1/8 tsp. pepper (freshly ground
   is best)
6 baked patty shells
1/2 C. shredded Cheddar cheese

Combine turkey and consomme in a saucepan; cook until turkey is thoroughly heated. Add next 7 ingredients, mixing well. Cook over low heat, stirring frequently, until mixture is thoroughly heated. Fill patty shells with hot turkey salad. Sprinkle with cheese, if desired, and bake at 350° for 5 minutes or until cheese melts. Serve immediately. Yield: 6 servings.

Great recipe for leftover turkey!

. . . hearts go home for the holidays

FRIED TURKEY

Betty Miller Wilkins - Prosperity, SC

1 Farm-Fresh turkey (any weight
   up to 18 lb.)
1/4 C. celery salt
1 onion
Liquid Crab Boil concentrate

1/4 C. cayenne pepper
1/4 C. garlic salt
5 gal. peanut oil
1/4 C. Accent
1/4 C. white pepper

Combine all seasonings except Crab Boil concentrate. Rinse turkey well in cold water; pat dry. Rub turkey well inside and out with seasoning mixture. Every 2 or so inches inject a solution of diluted Crab Boil into turkey (1 part Crab Boil, 4 parts water). Use a 35 or 50 CC hypodermic needle -- the kinds vets use for horses and which can be found at horse furnishings and supply stores. This will require 5 to 6 filled syringes. Put the whole onion inside the cavity. This should be done the day before and turkey allowed to marinate in refrigerator overnight. Heat oil to 375 to 400°. (You need to use a deep fat or candy thermometer.) Submerge turkey carefully in peanut oil and cook, maintaining temperature at 375° about 5 minutes per pound of turkey.

HURRY TURKEY CURRY

2 C. chopped cooked turkey (or hen)
1/2 C. chopped onion
2 tsp. curry powder
1 T. chopped almonds

1 C. sour cream
1 can cream of mushroom soup
1/4 C. sweet milk

Cook onions in butter until tender. Add almonds and saute lightly. Add mushroom soup diluted with 1/4 cup milk and sour cream. Stir until smooth and bubbling. Add curry powder and stir well. Add turkey. Cook all together about 20 minutes. Serve on rice.

THE BEST TURKEY SANDWICHES

2 slices fresh raisin bread
Shredded lettuce
Thinly sliced turkey

Thinly sliced jelled cranberry sauce
Mayonnaise
Prepared horseradish (optional)

Spread 2 slices of bread with mayonnaise (mixed with a small amount of prepared horseradish). Layer shredded lettuce, thinly sliced turkey and cranberry sauce on one slice; top with other slice. Cut in half.

Enjoy! You'll love it.

Note: A sandwich made with sliced turkey, mayonnaise and lots of salt and pepper on fresh white or wheat bread with a tall glass of cold milk is wonderful too.

TURKEY A LA LEFTOVER

1/4 C. butter or margarine
1/4 C. flour
1 1/2 C. milk
1/2 C. turkey or canned chicken broth
1 T. dry sherry

1 C. frozen green peas, thawed
1 3-oz. can sliced mushrooms, drained
1 pimiento, diced (1/2 of 4-oz. jar)
1 C. cooked turkey chunks
Hot cornbread, waffles or toast

In medium saucepan, melt butter and blend in flour until smooth. Slowly stir in milk, then broth and sherry. Cook and stir until thickened. Stir in peas, mushrooms, pimiento and turkey. Heat, stirring occasionally. Serve over cornbread. Serves 4.

"TURKEY IN A TENT"

Preheat oven to 325°. Line a roasting pan, at least 2" deep, with heavy duty aluminum foil. Remove neck and giblets from both cavities of defrosted turkey. Rinse turkey, pat dry and brush with vegetable oil. Insert meat thermometer into inner thigh for whole turkey or into thickest part of breast for turkey breast. Place turkey, breast side up, in foil-lined roasting pan. Place 1 apple, cut in quarters, 1 onion, halved, and 1 rib of celery inside turkey.

Make foil tent by tearing off a sheet of heavy duty aluminum foil. Crease foil crosswise through center. Place over turkey, leaving 1 to 2" between top of turkey and foil tent for heat circulation. Crimp foil onto long sides of pan to hold in place. Roast until meat thermometer reads 180 to 185° for whole turkey.

TURKEY PICCATA

1 lb. boneless turkey breast,
    skinned, sliced crosswise
    1/2" thick and pounded thin
Flour
2 T. butter or margarine, divided

2 T. oil, divided
Salt and pepper
2 T. lemon juice
1 lemon, cut in wedges

Coat turkey with flour. Heat 1 tablespoon each butter and oil in heavy skillet over high heat. Add turkey a few pieces at a time; quickly brown on both sides, adding more butter and oil if needed. Remove to warm platter. Sprinkle with salt, pepper and lemon juice. Garnish with lemon wedges. Makes 4 servings.

When frying chicken, dip first into ice cold buttermilk or water, then in flour or batter. Makes a crispy crust.

Turn a metal colander upside-down over skillet when frying chicken or any meat. The holes let the steam out, keeps the "splatters" in.

. . . hearts go home for the holidays

GLAZED GINGERED HAM (BAKED)

7 to 8 lb. fully cooked bone-in ham butt
6 C. unsifted all-purpose flour
2 T. ginger
1 T. ground cloves
1/2 tsp. salt

Preheat oven to 325°. Wipe ham with damp paper towels. In large bowl, combine flour, ginger, cloves, and salt; mix well. Gradually add 2 cups cold water, mixing well with fork. On lightly floured board, mold dough around top and side of ham until they are evenly covered. Place on rack in shallow roasting pan; insert meat thermometer in center away from bone. Bake until internal temperature is 130°, about 2 hours. Meanwhile, make Glaze.

Remove pastry covering from ham, and discard. With sharp knife, lift off skin. In outside fat layer, make diagonal cuts, 1 1/4" apart, to form a diamond pattern. Stud center of each diamond with a whole clove. Brush ham well with Glaze; bake 25 minutes, brushing twice more. Ham will be shiny. Makes 12 servings.

Glaze:
1 C. ginger ale
1 C. orange juice
1/2 C. light brown sugar, firmly packed
1 T. ginger
1 T. grated orange peel
About 24 whole cloves

Combine ingredients in small saucepan; bring to boiling, stirring. Reduce heat; simmer, uncovered, and stirring occasionally, 40 to 60 minutes. (Glaze should measure 1 cup.)

- DESSERTS -

HOLIDAY PECAN CAKE

2 C. butter or margarine, softened
4 1/2 C. sifted plain flour
1/4 tsp. salt
1 tsp. baking powder
6 eggs, separated
1 lb. light brown sugar
1/2 C. milk
1 tsp. vanilla extract
3 T. instant coffee dissolved in
   3 T. hot water
4 C. coarsely chopped pecans

Sift flour, salt and baking powder together. Separate yolks and whites of eggs. Beat egg whites until stiff. Set aside. Beat egg yolks until foamy. Cream butter and sugar in a large mixing bowl. Add beaten egg yolks. Mix well. Combine liquids (milk, vanilla and dissolved coffee). Add to butter mixture alternately with flour mixture, mixing well after each addition. Fold in pecans and beaten egg whites. Bake in 10" greased tube pan at 325° for 1½ hours. Let cool in pan placed on wire rack. Remove from pan; slice and serve with whipped cream or plain.

Note: Cake slices spread with a little butter and toasted are delicious too.

APPLE BUTTER YAM PIE

Nancy Hurley - Hartwell, GA

1 9" unbaked pastry shell
1 C. hot mashed sweet
   potatoes or yams
1/2 C. margarine or butter, softened
1/2 C. firmly packed light brown sugar
2 T. flour

1 15-oz. jar apple butter
1/2 C. milk
1/2 tsp. grated orange rind
1/2 tsp. salt
3 eggs
Whipped cream or nuts

Preheat oven to 400°. In large mixer bowl, beat yams, margarine, sugar and flour until well blended. Add apple butter, milk, rind, salt and eggs; beat well. Turn into pastry shell. Bake for 10 minutes, reduce oven temperature to 350°. Bake 50 minutes or longer until knife inserted near edge comes out clean. Cool. Serve with whipped cream and nuts.

Better than pumpkin or sweet potato pie.

TWO CHESS PIES

5 egg yolks
2 C. granulated sugar
1 T. cornmeal
1 tsp. vanilla

1 C. milk
1/2 C. butter, melted
1/2 tsp. nutmeg

Mix all ingredients in large bowl. Beat with wire whisk until smooth. Pour into 2 unbaked pie shells. Bake at 325° for 50 minutes. Makes 12 servings.

TWO COCONUT PIES

1 stick butter, softened
2 C. granulated sugar
3 1/2 T. all-purpose flour
1 1/2 C. milk (whole)

2 eggs, beaten
1 tsp. vanilla extract
1 tall can coconut
2 unbaked 9" pie shells

In a large bowl, cream butter, sugar and flour. Add milk, beaten eggs, vanilla and coconut. Stir well. Pour into 2 unbaked pie shells. Bake at 350° for 30 minutes. Makes 12 servings.

To keep a fluted pie crust from burning, wrap a piece of foil around edges while baking.

To prevent meringue from "pulling" when cutting, use a knife that has been sprayed lightly with cooking spray or rubbed lightly with butter.

MAPLE SUGAR PIE

Crust:

1 C. shredded rice cereal
1/4 C. granulated sugar
1/4 C. salted peanuts, finely chopped

1/4 C. butter, softened
2 tsp. hot water

Combine ingredients in order listed; mix well. Place in a buttered 9" pie plate. Pat on bottom and sides. Bake at 350° for 10 minutes. Cool.

Pie:

2/3 C. granulated sugar
1/4 C. cornstarch
1/2 tsp. salt
2 C. whole milk

1 C. maple syrup
3 egg yolks, beaten
1 T. butter
1/2 tsp. maple extract

In a saucepan, combine sugar, cornstarch and salt. Stir in milk and syrup. Cook over medium heat, stirring constantly, until mixture boils and becomes thick. Have egg yolks in a bowl and beat the hot mixture gradually into them. Pour egg yolk mixture into saucepan with other ingredients. Cook over low heat and stir until very thick. Then stir in butter and maple extract. Pour into unbaked crust. Chill 3 to 5 hours. Garnish with whipped cream and peanuts. Makes 6 to 8 servings.

Note: The back of a teaspoon works well when patting Crust into pie plate.

MANDARIN ORANGE PIE

2 cans Mandarin oranges, drained
   (reserve a few orange sections
   for garnish)
2 T. lemon juice

1 can sweetened condensed milk
1 9-oz. ctn. Cool Whip
1 10" graham cracker shell

Combine orange sections, lemon juice, condensed milk and Cool Whip. Mix well and pour into graham cracker crust. Garnish with reserved orange sections. Chill 3 to 6 hours. Slice and serve.

Note: This is a light and delicious dessert. Very good after a heavy meal.

BROWN SUGAR PUMPKIN PIE

3/4 C. brown sugar
1 env. gelatin
1/2 tsp. salt
1 tsp. cinnamon
1/2 tsp. nutmeg
1/4 tsp. ginger

3 slightly beaten egg yolks
3/4 C. milk
1 1/4 C. pumpkin
3 egg whites
1/3 C. granulated sugar

Combine brown sugar, gelatin, salt and spices. Combine egg yolks and milk. Stir into brown sugar mixture. Cook, stirring constantly, until it comes to a boil. Remove from heat; stir in pumpkin. Chill until mixture mounds slightly when spooned. Beat egg whites until soft peaks form. Fold pumpkin into egg whites. Turn into baked shell. Chill and garnish with whipped cream.

SPICED SWEET POTATO PIE

2 C. cooked sweet potatoes, mashed
2/3 C. packed light brown sugar
1 C. whipping cream
2 lg. eggs, beaten
1 tsp. ground cinnamon
1/2 tsp. ground ginger

1/2 tsp. nutmeg
1/4 tsp. allspice
1/8 tsp. ground cloves
1 unbaked 9" pie shell
Sweetened whipped cream,
    for garnish

In a large mixing bowl, combine all ingredients and pour into unbaked pie shell. Bake for 10 minutes at 450°. Reduce heat to 325° and bake 40 to 45 minutes more or until middle of pie is set. Cool on a wire rack. Serve garnished with a dollop of whipped cream. Makes 8 servings.

Leftovers (if any) should be refrigerated.

DATE-RAISIN-NUT COOKIES

1 C. flour
1 tsp. baking powder
1/4 tsp. salt
1/2 C. butter or margarine, softened
1 C. nuts, chopped fine
1 C. flaked sweetened or
    unsweetened coconut

1/2 C. packed finely cut up
    pitted dates
1/2 C. raisins
1 egg, beaten
2 tsp. brandy or bourbon (optional)

In bowl, mix flour, baking powder and salt. Cut in butter until particles are size of peas. Stir in nuts, coconut, dates, raisins, egg and brandy. Mix with wooden spoon until dough forms. Chill 1 hour. Shape in 1" balls. Place 1/2" apart on greased cookie sheet. With tines of fork dipped in flour, flatten balls to form 1 1/2" cookies. Bake in preheated 350° oven for 15 minutes or until golden brown. Makes 48.

CARROT CAKE SQUARES

2 C. flour
2 C. sugar
1 tsp. salt
2 tsp. soda
2 tsp. cinnamon

1 1/2 C. oil
4 eggs
3 C. shredded carrots
1 C. chopped nuts

Sift dry ingredients; add oil and eggs. Stir in carrots and nuts. Spread in greased and floured jelly-roll pan. Bake at 350° for 35 minutes. Spread Frosting over cooled cake. Cut into squares. Yield: 3 dozen.

Frosting:
1/4 C. margarine
1/2 tsp. vanilla
1 3-oz. pkg. cream cheese

1 1/2 C. powdered sugar
1/8 tsp. salt

Beat together all ingredients.

FROSTED PUMPKIN BARS

4 eggs, beaten
1 C. oil
2 C. sugar
1 C. pumpkin
1/2 tsp. salt

2 tsp. cinnamon
1 tsp. soda
1 tsp. baking powder
2 C. flour
1 C. chopped nuts or raisins (optional)

Combine all ingredients, mixing well. Spread in a greased and floured jelly-roll pan. Bake at 350° for 25 minutes. Cool slightly. Spread Frosting over warm bars. Yield: 3 dozen.

Frosting:
1 3-oz. pkg. cream cheese, softened
6 T. butter, softened
3/4 lb. powdered sugar

1 tsp. vanilla
1 tsp. milk (more, if needed)

Combine ingredients, add more milk if needed for desired consistency.

AUTUMN BUTTERSCOTCH CUPS (FOR ICE CREAM)

1 12-oz. pkg. butterscotch morsels
12 cupcake paper liners (3 to 4")

Butter pecan or pralines and
    cream ice cream
Pecan halves, for garnish

In top of double boiler, melt butterscotch morsels. Place paper liners in muffin tins. With a rubber spatula, coat inside of papers with melted butterscotch. Refrigerate until ready to use. To serve, remove papers and fill with 2 scoops butter pecan or praline and cream ice cream. Garnish with pecan half. Serve on a lace paper doily-lined dessert plate.

CRANBERRY SUNDAES

1 C. sugar
2 C. fresh cranberries
1 T. grated orange peel
1/2 C. broken walnuts

3 T. light corn syrup
2 T. cointreau
1 qt. vanilla ice cream

In medium saucepan, combine sugar and 1 cup water; heat, stirring, to dissolve sugar. Bring to boiling; boil, uncovered, and without stirring 10 minutes or until syrup thickens slightly. Wash and drain cranberries, removing any stems. Add cranberries, orange peel and walnuts to sugar syrup. Cook gently until cranberries begin to burst, about 5 minutes. Remove from heat; stir in corn syrup and cointreau. Refrigerate. Serve cold over ice cream.

PUMPKIN WALNUT CHEESECAKE
Nancy Hurley - Hartwell, GA

Crust:

1 1/2 C. crushed vanilla wafers
1/4 C. granulated sugar

6 T. melted butter

Combine all ingredients. Press firmly into bottom and halfway up sides of lightly greased 9" springform pan.

Filling:

3 8-oz. pkg. cream cheese,
   room temperature
3/4 C. granulated sugar
3/4 C. brown sugar, firmly packed
5 eggs
1/4 C. heavy cream

1 tsp. cinnamon
1/2 tsp. nutmeg
1/4 tsp. cloves
1 lb. pumpkin (canned or
   freshly cooked)

Cream cheese; add sugars and beat until light and fluffy. Add eggs, 1 at a time, beating well after each addition. Stir in cream, spices and pumpkin. Pour into prepared cheesecake pan. Bake in a preheated 350° oven for 1 hour.

Topping:

6 T. butter
1 C. brown sugar, firmly packed

1 C. coarsely chopped walnuts

Cream butter and brown sugar. Stir in walnuts. When Filling is out of oven, spoon Topping gently on top. Bake for 15 minutes more. Cool completely, then refrigerate overnight. Serves at least 12. (You can get 16 slices easily.) Put a dollop of whipped cream on top and grind fresh nutmeg over cream before serving.

This is wonderful!

RAISIN RICE PUDDING

4 C. whole milk
1/2 tsp. salt
2/3 C. sugar
1/2 tsp. nutmeg

1/4 tsp. cinnamon
3 to 4 T. rice (long grain - uncooked)
1/2 C. raisins

Preheat oven to 300°. Mix all ingredients together in a large bowl. Pour into a buttered baking dish. Bake at 300° for approximately 3½ hours. Stir several times during first hour or so of cooking. Serve with rich cream, Makes approximately 8 servings.

Note: May be baked in 8 individual custard cups as well.

- SAUCES -

BUTTERSCOTCH CREAM SAUCE

2 C. brown sugar, packed   1/2 C. Half and Half
1 stick butter

  Combine all ingredients in a heavy saucepan. Boil without stirring for 5 minutes.
Serve hot or cold. Makes approximately 1 cup.
  Good on any dessert.

CARAMEL SAUCE

2 C. granulated sugar   2 C. whipping cream
1 C. light corn syrup   Pinch of salt
1 1/2 sticks butter or margarine   1 tsp. vanilla

  Heat in a heavy saucepan over medium heat. Bring to a boil. Stir all the while.
Reduce heat to have a very slow boil and cook 30 minutes. Stir often. When caramel
colored, stir in vanilla. Makes approximately 4 cups.
  Keeps 2 months in refrigerator. Makes nice gifts in decorative jars. Serve hot or
cold.

HONEY/ORANGE SAUCE

1 C. honey (light)   1/2 C. orange juice
1/4 C. chopped orange peel   Pinch of salt
   (use a vegetable grater)

  Combine all ingredients. Let stand in bowl over hot, not boiling water for 30 minutes.
Serve on gingerbread, pudding or ice cream.

Do not grease the sides of cake pans; grease only the bottom. This allows batter
to "climb" up the sides.

To cut calories and fat, use evaporated skim milk or plain yogurt instead of
heavy cream.

. . . hearts go home for the holidays

Christmas

- PARTY FOODS -

CHRISTMAS POTPOURRI (NON-EDIBLE)

3 C. fresh juniper sprigs with berries
2 C. red rosebuds
1 C. bay leaves
1/4 C. cinnamon chips
2 T. cloves
10 drops rose oil

3 drops pine oil
6 drops cinnamon oil
1 T. orrisroot chips
5 whole dried rose blossoms
3 (3") cinnamon sticks
20 assorted pine cones, painted gold

Combine the juniper, rosebuds, bay leaves, cinnamon chips, cloves and cones in a big ceramic bowl. In a separate dish, mix the oils, with the orrisroot. Stir this mixture into the first one and put into a closed container to mellow for a few weeks, stirring occasionally. Place the potpourri in a dish and scatter the rose blossoms and cinnamon sticks on top.

COOKIE DECORATIONS (NON-EDIBLE)

Dough:
1 C. cornstarch
2 C. baking soda

1 1/4 C. cold water

Paint:
1 egg yolk
1 T. water

Desired food coloring

Stir cornstarch and baking soda together in a saucepan. Add water and stir until smooth. Cook over medium heat, stirring until mixture resembles dry mashed potatoes. Pour into a plate. Cover with damp towel. Cool. Coat a flat surface with cornstarch and knead dough until smooth. Roll out on cornstarch coated surface. Cut in desired shapes with cookie cutters dipped in cornstarch. Let dry on wax paper. Decorate with paint as desired.

Note: If planning to hang on a tree, cut a hole with a plastic straw 1/2" from top before drying. These may also be glued to wreaths, etc.

SIMMERING SPICE (NON-EDIBLE)

3 sticks cinnamon
3 bay leaves
1 qt. water

1/4 C. whole cloves
1/2 lemon, cut in 2 pieces
1/2 orange, cut in 2 pieces

In a saucepan, combine all ingredients. Bring to a boil and then simmer. Your house will smell wonderful and inviting.

CHEESE PUFFS (EASY) (HAL'S FAVORITE)

2 sticks margarine (softened)
2 C. grated sharp cheese
2 1/2 C. self-rising flour

2 C. Rice Krispie cereal
Dash of red pepper or hot sauce*

*Not too much or they'll be too hot!

Mix all ingredients. Form into small balls. Place slightly apart on cookie sheet and flatten with fork dipped in water. Bake at 325° until done.

Good! Good! Good!

CROCKED CHEESE

1/2 lb. finely grated extra sharp
   Cheddar cheese
3 T. butter

2 to 3 T. port wine or cream sherry
Dash of nutmeg

Cream the butter and cheese; add other ingredients. Mix until well blended. Pack in a crockery container. Refrigerate. This recipe makes approximately 2 1/2 cups.

Serve at room temperature with crackers.

HAM & CHEESE ROLLS

1 8-oz. pkg. cream cheese,
   at room temperature

1 12-oz. pkg. Danish ham
1 T. chopped chives

Separate slices of ham. Cream cheese and chopped chives. Spread mixture on each ham slice (one at a time) and roll jelly-roll style. Place each rolled up slice "seam" side down on a plate and refrigerate until cheese has firmed again. Slice into 1/2" pinwheels. Serve on a glass plate, garnished with sprig of parsley or cilantro.

NOEL WREATH (EDIBLE)

1 10-oz. pkg. lg. marshmallows
1/3 C. butter or margarine

1 (5 1/2-oz.) pkg. toasted rice cereal
Cinnamon candies or small gumdrops

In top of double boiler, over boiling water, melt marshmallows with butter, stirring occasionally. Pour marshmallow mixture over cereal in large, well-buttered bowl. Mix with wooden spoon until all of cereal is coated. With buttered hands, press mixture firmly into a 5½-cup ring mold. Refrigerate 10 minutes. Run spatula around edge of mold to loosen; turn out onto wax paper lined tray; cover with wax paper. Let stand overnight at room temperature to harden. To decorate: Attach a bright green bow to wreath. Dot with candies to resemble ornaments. Makes 14 to 16 servings.

A beautiful centerpiece at Christmas or anytime is simply a glass bowl of red and green apples.

Good ideas for place cards: Write names in icing on homemade or bought sugar cookies. Use glass balls with names on them. Tie a festive bow through hanger. Use small greeting cards as each place with name on envelope.

COCKTAIL QUAIL

6 to 8 quail	Butter
Vermouth or dry white wine	Sugar
Fresh mushrooms	Cinnamon
Garlic salt	Nutmeg

Separate legs and breasts of quail to make the pieces a suitable size for appetizers. Saute quail parts in butter. Season to taste with garlic salt and freshly ground pepper. After quail is fully browned (do not overcook as additional cooking will take place when heating for serving), marinate for 24 hours in vermouth or dry white wine adding to taste a dash of sugar, cinnamon and nutmeg.

Before serving, heat at 250° for 1 hour, and add sliced, fresh mushrooms and 1 stick of butter.

Can be prepared ahead of time.

SMOKED SALMON ROLL-UPS

3 T. sour cream	1/8 tsp. pepper
1 8-oz. pkg. cream cheese	1/4 tsp. salt
2 tsp. chopped dill (fresh) or	Thin slices of smoked salmon
1 tsp. dried dill	

Combine sour cream, cream cheese, dill, pepper and salt. Mix well until spreading consistency. Spread on each slice of smoked salmon. Roll up jelly-roll style. Chill and slice 1/2" thick.

SAUSAGE BALLS

Lynda Rogers - Manchester, GA

1 lb. Cracker Barrel brand sharp cheese, grated	1 lb. mild or hot sausage
	3 C. Bisquick mix

Mix well all ingredients. Roll into small balls. Bake on ungreased cookie sheet at 400° for 15 minutes.

SAUSAGE PINWHEELS

2 C. self-rising flour	2/3 C. milk
1/4 C. shortening	3/4 lb. ground hot pork sausage

Place flour in a medium bowl; cut in shortening with a pastry blender until mixture is crumbly. Add milk, stirring with a fork until dry ingredients are moistened. Turn dough out onto a lightly floured surface; knead lightly 3 or 4 times. Roll dough into a 12x9" rectangle. Spread uncooked sausage (at room temperature) over dough, leaving a 1/2" border. Roll up, jelly-roll fashion, starting at long side; pinch seam to seal. Wrap in plastic wrap, and refrigerate several hours.

Unwrap and cut roll into 1/4" slices, and place 1" apart on lightly greased baking sheets. Bake at 450° for 12 to 14 minutes or until pinwheels are golden brown. Serve warm or at room temperature. Yield: About 3 1/2 dozen.

SAUSAGE ROLLS

8 oz. puff pastry (your favorite recipe)
3/4 lb. bulk sausage

A little beaten egg or milk

Roll pastry out into oblong shape. Cut into strips about 3 1/2" wide and 2 1/2" long. Divide the sausage into 6 to 8 even pieces. Roll into 2 1/2" long shapes to fit just inside the edges of each piece of pastry. Place roll of sausage into center of pastry. Fold pastry in half over sausage, dampening inside of one edge just slightly and press the edges together with flat side of fork tine. Make 2 or 3 little slits with a sharp knife across top. Bake on top rack of oven at 445° for 15 to 20 minutes. Serve hot.

SHRIMP CHRISTMAS TREE
Beatrice McCurry Miller - Charleston, SC
(One of the Twelve)

2 lb. med. shrimp, fresh or frozen
1 1/2 qt. water
1/3 C. salt
3 bunches curly endive

1 styrofoam cone, 1 1/2 feet high
1 sm. bx. round toothpicks
Cocktail Sauce

Thaw frozen shrimp. Place shrimp in boiling, salted water. Cover and simmer about 5 minutes or until shrimp are pink and tender. Drain. Peel shrimp, leaving the tail section of the shell on. Remove sand veins and wash. Chill. Separate and wash endive. Chill. Starting at the base of the styrofoam cone and working up, cover the cone with overlapping leaves of endive. Fasten endive to the cone with toothpick halves. Cover fully with greens to resemble Christmas tree. Attach shrimp to tree with toothpicks. Provide Cocktail Sauce for dunking. Makes 8 to 10 servings.

Cocktail Sauce:
1 1/2 C. catsup
1 T. lemon juice
1 T. Worcestershire sauce
2 T. horseradish

1 1/2 tsp. sugar
Generous dash of liquid
** hot pepper sauce**
Salt and pepper, to taste

Combine all ingredients and chill.
Variation: You may use meats such as rolled up ham, and cookie cutter cutouts of salami and bologna or cubes of semi-hard cheese attached to "tree" with toothpicks.

SPINACH BALLS

2 10-oz. pkg. chopped spinach,
** cooked and drained well**
2 C. seasoned stuffing mix
3/4 C. softened butter

1 C. grated Parmesan cheese
6 eggs, well beaten
Salt and pepper, to taste

Combine all ingredients, then shape into balls (about the size of a walnut). Freeze in a single layer. Bake frozen on a cookie sheet 1" apart at 350° for 10 to 12 minutes.

SPINACH DIP

1 pkg. chopped spinach, thawed
    and drained (do not cook)
1 C. mayonnaise
1/4 C. parsley flakes

1 sm. grated onion
1 tsp. seasoned salt
1 tsp. paprika

Squeeze excess water out of spinach. Mix spinach with all other ingredients. Chill 1 or 2 hours. Serve.

STUFFED COCKTAIL TOMATOES

Stuffing:
3/4 C. shredded Cheddar cheese
1/8 tsp. garlic salt

1/4 C. stuffed pimientos, chopped
1/8 tsp. fresh ground pepper

Parsley sprigs, to garnish

8 to 10 sm. tomatoes

Combine stuffing ingredients in a bowl. Wash tomatoes; pat dry. Place stem side down and make 2 criss-cross cuts (not all the way through to bottom). Stuff with Stuffing. Stick a small sprig of parsley in top. Cover with plastic wrap and chill.

- BEVERAGES -

BURGUNDY PUNCH

2 12-oz. cans frozen white grape juice
7 C. cold water

2/3 C. lemon juice
2 bot. sparkling red grape juice

Combine ingredients. Pour punch over Ice Ring in punch bowl and serve immediately. Makes 16 servings.

Ice Ring*:
1 bot. 7-Up
1 bunch red grapes

Sprigs of mint
Ring mold

*Make Ice Ring ahead 1 day.
Pour 1/2 of 7-Up in ice mold. Freeze. Place grapes and mint sprigs (in small clusters) in ring mold and pour remaining 7-Up over grapes and mint. Cover with plastic wrap and freeze.

MULLED CHAMPAGNE PUNCH

Combine 1/2 quart each pineapple juice, grapefruit juice, and apple juice, 1/2 can frozen lemonade concentrate, 1/4 cup sugar and 1/2 tablespoon mulling spices. Mix until sugar and concentrate are dissolved. Chill for at least 10 hours to allow spices to draw. To serve, remove spices, stir in 1 1/2 quarts ginger ale and 1 bottle champagne. Garnish with fresh fruit slices. Makes 1 1/4 gallons or 35 (4-ounce servings).

HOT CRANBERRY PUNCH

2 6-oz. cans frozen lemonade
   concentrate
2 pt. bot. cranberry juice cocktail

1/2 tsp. ground allspice
1/4 tsp. ground cinnamon
2 1/2 C. water

Combine all ingredients in a large saucepan. Heat to just before boiling point. Reduce heat and simmer for 10 minutes. Serve hot. Makes 2 quarts.

PEPPERMINT-EGGNOG PUNCH

1 pt. soft pink peppermint stick
   ice cream
2 C. dairy eggnog
1 (1-pt. 12-oz.) bot. club soda, chilled
Few drops red food color

1 C. heavy cream, whipped
16 red peppermint sticks
1/3 C. crushed peppermint sticks
   (optional)

Spoon ice cream into punch bowl. Add eggnog and club soda, mixing well. Stir in food color, to tint slightly pink. Spoon whipped cream over surface. Put peppermint stick stirrer in each punch cup. Top each serving with a little of the crushed peppermint sticks. Makes 16 (4-ounce) servings.

WASSAIL BOWL
Betty Wilkins - Prosperity, SC

Whole cloves
6 med. oranges
10 (2") cinnamon sticks
1 gal. apple cider

1 1/2 C. lemon juice
2 C. vodka
1/4 C. brandy

Insert cloves in oranges about 1/2" apart. Bake uncovered in a shallow pan for 30 minutes at 350°. While the oranges are baking, heat the cider in a large pot until bubbles appear around edge. Remove from heat. Add lemon juice, cinnamon sticks and oranges. Cover and simmer over very low heat for 30 minutes. Add the vodka and brandy. Pour into a large heated punch bowl and serve warm.

For a festive punch, surround base of punch bowl with holly or magnolia leaves and 5 or 6 votive candles in glass holders.

- SOUPS -

EAST BAY BROCCOLI BISQUE

1 14-oz. can chicken broth
2 10-oz. pkg. frozen chopped broccoli
  (uncooked)
1 bay leaf
1/4 C. butter

1/4 C. flour (all-purpose)
1/4 tsp. salt
Dash of pepper
2 C. Half and Half cream
1/4 tsp. ground mace

Combine broth and broccoli in a saucepan; add bay leaf and bring to a boil. Reduce heat and simmer for 5 minutes. Melt butter; add flour, salt, pepper and ground mace. Cook until bubbly; gradually add cream, stirring until a smooth sauce. Remove from heat. Remove bay leaf from broth mixture. In a blender, puree broth and broccoli until smooth. Add to cream sauce and heat. Serve hot with croutons cut in small circles like wreaths. Garnish with paprika. Yield: 6 cups.

CHRISTMAS CLAM CHOWDER

2 C. fresh minced clams or
  2 cans minced clams
2 potatoes, diced
6 strips bacon, diced
2 sm. onions, diced
1 T. butter
1 qt. milk

1 can condensed milk or
  1 pt. Half and Half
1 stick butter
Chopped parsley
1 tsp. Tabasco sauce
1/8 tsp. garlic salt
Salt and pepper, to taste
Paprika, to garnish

Fry diced bacon and onions in butter until browned. Cook diced potatoes in just enough water to cover until tender. Add bacon and onion (with drippings). Add clams and butter. Combine milk and condensed milk. Add to clam mixture. Simmer for 10 minutes; do not boil. Stir; add seasonings and Tabasco sauce. Serve in heated bowls, garnished with parsley and paprika.

Note: Stir during simmering time to prevent burning.

CRAB BISQUE

1 can tomato soup
1 can split pea soup
2 C. beef broth
1/2 lb. crab meat

1/2 C. cream
Sherry
Salt and pepper
Sprigs of parsley, for garnish

Mix soups; bring to a boil. Add crab meat and cream. Reduce to simmer for 3 to 5 minutes. Season with sherry, salt and pepper. Serve in heated bowls. Garnish with sprigs of parsley.

For simple brown roux, heat 2 tablespoons shortening in skillet; add 2 tablespoons flour, salt and pepper to taste. Stir well. Use as base for soups, stews and gumbo.

- SALADS -

AMBROSIA SALAD

1 can Mandarin oranges, drained
1 can pineapple chunks, drained
1 C. miniature marshmallows

1 can flaked coconut
1/2 pt. sour cream

Cut orange sections and pineapple chunks in half. Mix all ingredients. Refrigerate overnight. If desired, reserve a small amount of coconut for a garnish with cherry. Yield: 4 servings.

ASPARAGUS AND PEPPER SALAD

1 #2 can asparagus spears, drained
1/2 green pepper

1/2 red pepper

Drain stalks of canned asparagus. Cut green or red peppers in rings 1/3" wide. Place 3 or 4 stalks in each ring and serve chilled on lettuce leaves with French dressing.

ROYAL CRANBERRY SALAD

1 pkg. Royal raspberry Jell-O
1 1/2 C. boiling water
1 orange, seeds removed

1 16-oz. can whole cranberry sauce
1 T. lemon juice

In a small saucepan, dissolve Jell-O in boiling water. Remove from heat. Set aside and cool 10 minutes. In a food processor or blender, place orange (seeds removed) sections with peeling and cranberry sauce. Mix until orange is in very small pieces. Add Jell-O mixture and lemon juice; mix well and pour into a mold (or individual molds) which have been very thinly coated with mayonnaise. Chill until firm. Cut in squares and serve on lettuce.

CHRISTMAS SLAW (RED AND GREEN)

First Mixture:
1/2 green cabbage, shredded
1/2 red cabbage, shredded
1/2 C. green pepper, chopped fine

1/2 C. red pepper, chopped fine
1 med. onion, chopped fine

Combine all ingredients in a large bowl. Make the following Dressing:

Dressing:
1/2 C. mayonnaise
1/2 C. sour cream
1 tsp. seasoned salt
2 tsp. sugar

1 1/2 tsp. vinegar
1 tsp. lemon juice
1/4 tsp. ground black pepper

MIx ingredients well and fold into slaw mixture. Chill for several hours.

CORN RELISH

2 C. cooked fresh corn kernels or
   1 10-oz. pkg. frozen corn
   kernels, cooked according
   to package directions
1/3 C. chopped zucchini (optional)

1/4 C. chopped sweet red pepper
2 T. chopped red onion
Parsley Dressing
Lettuce leaves

Combine corn, zucchini, red pepper and onion in bowl. Pour on dressing, toss. Refrigerate, covered, until serving. Drain corn salad. Place lettuce leaves on plates; spoon on corn mixture.

Parsley Dressing:
Whisk together 2 tablespoons cider vinegar, 1 tablespoon vegetable oil, 1 tablespoon finely chopped parsley, 1 1/2 teaspoons sugar, 1/4 teaspoon salt, 1/4 teaspoon chili powder and 1/8 teaspoon pepper in small bowl.

DELLA ROBBIA SALAD PLATTER

1 (1-lb. 13-oz.) can pear halves
   (about 8)
1 (8 1/2-oz.) can pineapple slices
1 1-lb. can peach halves
1 1-lb. jar spiced crab apples
1 (12 1/2-oz.) jar kumquats

2 3-oz. pkg. cream cheese
2 T. chopped walnuts
1 bunch watercress
Lg. pitted dates
Pecan halves
Della Robbia Salad Dressing

Refrigerate the pear halves, pineapple slices, peach halves, crab apples, and kumquats until well chilled, about 2 hours. Drain each well. Meanwhile, let cream cheese stand in small bowl, at room temperature, until very soft. Add walnuts; mix well. Using cream cheese mixture, put pear halves together, making 4 whole pears. (If desired, put more cream cheese through pastry tube, to decorate pear seams.) Wash watercress; drain, remove long stems. Around edge of large, round platter, arrange watercress sprigs to form a wreath. On wreath, place whole pears alternately with pineapple slices. Top each pineapple slice with peach half, rounded side up. On outer edge of wreath, place 1 crab apple between each whole pear and pineapple slice. On inner edge of wreath, place 2 kumquats opposite each crab apple. Here and there, group several dates and pecans. Refrigerate until serving time. Serve with Della Robbia Salad Dressing. Makes 8 servings.

Della Robbia Salad Dressing:
1/2 C. apricot nectar
2 T. lemon juice
1/2 C. salad oil

1/2 tsp. sugar
1/4 tsp. salt
1/4 C. crumbled Roquefort cheese

Combine all ingredients in jar with tight-fitting lid; shake vigorously to combine. Makes 1 1/4 cups.

DIVINITY SALAD

1 #2 can sliced pineapple, cut up
1 C. chopped nuts
1/2 lb. marshmallows, cut up

1/2 pt. whipping cream
2 egg whites

Sauce:
3 T. vinegar
1 T. sugar
3 T. pineapple juice

1/2 tsp. powdered mustard
1/2 tsp. salt
2 egg yolks

Cook Sauce and let cool.
Add cooled sauce to pineapple and marshmallows. Cover and let stand 6 hours or overnight. Before serving, whip cream and egg whites and mix with other ingredients. Add nuts.

MERRY CHRISTMAS SALAD

1 lg. ctn. Cool Whip
1 can sweetened condensed milk,
    chilled
1 can fruit cocktail, drained and chilled

1 can crushed pineapple,
    drained and chilled
1 C. pecans, chopped
1 can cherry pie filling, chilled

Place all ingredients (separately) in refrigerator and chill. Mix Cool Whip and milk. Fold in fruit cocktail, pineapple, nuts and pie filling. Pour into large casserole dish. Refrigerate overnight.

RED & GREEN SALAD

1 3-oz. pkg. sun-dried tomatoes
1 C. boiling water
1 cucumber, sliced thin
8 C. fresh spinach

1 sm. onion, sliced into thin rings
1 C. fresh mushrooms, sliced
1/4 C. grated Parmesan or
    Cheddar cheese

Put boiling water over sun-dried tomatoes; set aside. Combine remaining ingredients. Add drained tomatoes. Top with Dressing.

Dressing:
1/2 C. olive oil
1 tsp. honey Dijon mustard

1/2 tsp. salt
1/4 tsp. pepper

Makes 8 to 10 servings.

Cut up salad greens in fairly large pieces with scissors. Drain well so that dressing will adhere.

Try salad greens other than a head of lettuce for salad: endive, escarole, romaine, leaf lettuce, spinach, etc. Wash and drain or spin dry.

Rub or season salad bowl with peeled clove of garlic before making salad. This adds a lovely flavor.

. . . hearts go home for the holidays

TROPICAL SHRIMP SALAD

8 pineapple rings
8 lettuce leaves
1 lg. green pepper, cut in 1/2" rings

1 1/2 lb. boiled shrimp,
　peeled and chopped
1 lg. rib celery, chopped finely
French or Russian dressing

On each leaf of lettuce, place a pineapple ring, then a pepper ring. Fill the pepper ring with shrimp mixed with celery. Pour dressing over shrimp mixture. Chill and serve with crisp crackers. Garnish with a thin twist of lemon. Makes 8 servings.

- BREADS -

CHRISTMAS CRANBERRY BREAD

2 1/4 C. flour
2 tsp. baking powder
1/2 tsp. salt
3/4 C. packed brown sugar
2 T. butter or margarine
1 egg, beaten
1 C. ground or chopped raw
　cranberries (can be
　ground in blender)

1/2 C. orange marmalade
1/4 C. boiling water
1 tsp. baking soda
1/2 C. chopped pecans
1/2 C. golden raisins
Confectioner's sugar frosting
　(optional)

Stir together flour, baking powder and salt; set aside. Cream sugar and butter until fluffy. Stir in egg and cranberries. Blend marmalade, water and soda, then stir into creamed mixture. Stir in flour mixture until well blended. Stir in pecans and raisins. Turn into 2 greased 8x4x2" loaf pans and bake in 325° oven for 50 minutes or until pick inserted in center comes out clean. Cool pans on rack 10 minutes, then invert on racks, turning loaves top side up. When cool, wrap airtight in foil or plastic and store overnight in cool dry place; will keep about 1 week.

Decorate with confectioner's sugar frosting before giving.

Cabbage when slightly parboiled and drained, then cooked in waterless cookware makes a great salad with French dressing or a vegetable dish with tomato sauce.

For quick and easy coleslaw: Mix 1 cup mayonnaise with 1 medium shredded green cabbage. Chill and serve. Add salt and pepper to taste.

A half hour or longer in the refrigerator makes biscuit, cookie or pie crust dough easier to handle. Eliminates having to use so much flour on the board which tends to toughen dough.

For easy poached egg, place 1/2 cup water in a glass measuring cup. Heat for 1 1/2 minutes on full power in microwave. Remove from oven. Crack egg and place it in heated water. Pierce the egg yolk with a fork tine. Microwave on full power for 30 to 45 seconds. Drain in a slotted kitchen spoon and slice onto toasted bread or an English muffin. Try this a few times to decide what cooking time gives you desired results.

TWILA'S CHRISTMAS COFFEE CAKE
Twila Bowen - Manchester, GA

1 pkg. yeast
1/4 C. warm water
2 1/4 C. all-purpose flour
2 T. sugar
1 tsp. salt

1/2 C. margarine or butter, softened
1/4 C. Pet evaporated milk
1 unbeaten egg
1/4 C. currants or chopped raisins
   (I prefer currants)

Dissolve yeast in warm water; set aside. Sift together flour, sugar and salt. Cut in margarine or butter. Stir in egg and currants or raisins. Add dissolved yeast. Mix well. Cover and chill 2 hours or overnight. After the dough has chilled, mix Filling together and set aside. Divide dough into 3 equal pieces; roll out each on a floured surface into 12x6" rectangle. Spread each with with 1/3 of Filling. Roll up jelly-roll style; seal edges. Place on a very lightly greased cookie sheet. Shape each into a crescent. Cut slits on ouside edge at 1" intervals (do cut all the way through). Let rise for 45 minutes in warm place covered with towel. Bake at 350° for 25 to 30 minutes. Glaze while hot. Makes 3.

Wonderul served immediately or reheated.

Filling:
1/4 C. butter or margarine, melted
1/2 C. brown sugar, packed

1/2 C. chopped pecans

Combine ingredients.

Glaze:
Brown 2 tablespoons butter. Stir in 1 cup powdered sugar and 1/2 teaspoon vanilla. Add evaporated milk until spreadable consistency.

For holidays, use 1/2 cup chopped red and/or green cherries. For Valentine, you can shape into a heart.

BUTTERMILK BISCUITS

1 3/4 C. all-purpose flour, sifted
1 tsp. salt
3 tsp. baking powder
1 tsp. sugar

1/2 tsp. baking soda
5 T. butter
2/3 to 3/4 C. buttermilk

Sift flour before measuring. Add other dry ingredients and then sift again. Cut in butter. Add milk to form a soft dough. Pat out on a floured board to 1/2" thickness. Cut out and arrange on an ungreased baking sheet. Bake 12 to 15 minutes at 450°. Makes 2 dozen biscuits, about 1 1/2" wide.

Note: This recipe is good for making ham biscuits.

TIPSY ANGELS

1 20-oz. pkg. Bisquick mix
1 can beer, at room temperature

2 T. sugar

Mix and let stand for 30 minutes. Spoon into greased muffin tin. Bake at 375° for 20 minutes or at 425° for 10 minutes.

HERBED CORNBREAD DRESSING

2 T. butter
1 med. onion, chopped
1 C. celery, diced
6 C. cold cornbread cubes
2 C. bread cubes
2 C. chicken broth

2 tsp. dried sage leaves, crumbled
1/2 tsp. salt
1/4 tsp. ground black pepper
1/2 C. chopped fresh parsley
2 eggs, beaten

In a large pot, saute onion and celery in butter until tender. Remove from heat and stir in remaining ingredients. Bake at 350° loosely covered with foil for 15 minutes and uncovered for 15 more minutes.

CRUNCHY CROUTONS

1/4 C. Parmesan cheese, grated
2 T. oregano
2 tsp. garlic powder
1 T. basil
1/2 tsp. seasoned salt or salt

1/2 tsp. ground pepper or
   freshly ground pepper
5 C. dried bread cubes
3 T. olive oil

In one bowl, combine cheese and spices. In another large bowl, toss bread cubes with olive oil. Add spices and cheese. Mix well. Spread on ungreased baking sheet. Cook completely at 225° for 1 hour. Stir while baking so that cubes toast on all sides. Cool completely. Store in airtight container or Ziploc bags. Keeps 1 month.
   Good with salad and soups.

- SIDE DISHES -

CHANTILLY APPLESAUCE WITH HORSERADISH

3 C. applesauce
1/2 C. granulated sugar

2 T. prepared horseradish
4 or 5 T. whipped cream

Combine first 3 ingredients in order listed. Chill. Fold in whipped cream just before serving.
   Good with roasted turkey or chicken.

BUFFET BRUSSELS SPROUTS

2 lb. fresh Brussels sprouts
1/2 C. butter or margarine
1 C. coarsely chopped pecans

1 2-oz. jar diced pimiento, drained
1/4 C. minced fresh parsley
2 T. lemon juice

Cover and cook Brussels sprouts in a small amount of salted water for 5 to 8 minutes or until tender. Drain and place in a serving dish; keep warm. Melt butter in a skillet over medium heat; add pecans and saute until butter is golden and pecans are lightly toasted. Remove from heat; stir in remaining ingredients. Pour over Brussels sprouts and serve immediately. Makes 12 servings.

BRANDIED CRANBERRIES

3 12-oz. pkg. (about 9 C.) fresh
   cranberries

3 C. sugar
1/2 C. brandy

Place cranberries evenly in a single layer in two lightly greased jelly-roll pans; pour sugar evenly over cranberries. Cover tightly with aluminum foil; bake at 350° for 1 hour. Spoon cranberries into a large serving bowl; add brandy and mix well. Cool completely. Serve at room temperature or refrigerate up to 1 week and serve chilled. Makes 12 servings.

CRANBERRY YAM CRUNCH

2 17-oz. cans yams, drained
2 C. fresh cranberries
1/2 C. all-purpose flour
1/2 C. brown sugar (packed)
1/2 C. oatmeal (quick-cooking or
   old fashioned)

1 tsp. cinnamon
1/4 tsp. ground cloves
1/3 C. butter or margarine,
   cut in small pieces
2 C. miniature marshmallows

Preheat oven to 350°. In a mixing bowl, combine yams with cranberries. Mix lightly. In another bowl, combine flour, brown sugar, oats, cinnamon, cloves and margarine. Stir until butter is mixed into other ingredients. Remove 1 cup of mixture and stir into yams and cranberries. Pour into a buttered 9x13" casserole dish. Sprinkle remaining crumb mixture over top and bake at 350° for 30 to 35 minutes. Add marshmallows (spread evenly) and broil about 2 minutes. Watch carefully so marshmallows don't burn. Makes 6 to 8 servings.

GREEN BEANS AND PEPPER RINGS

2 cans whole green beans or
   2 lb. whole fresh
   green beans, cooked

2 med. red peppers

Cut red pepper into 1/3 to 1/2" wide rings. Remove seeds and veins. Heat canned beans or cook fresh green beans. Divide into 8 equal bunches and slip each bunch through pepper ring. Keep warm until ready to serve.

These are very pretty on a platter or individual plates.

Note: Add enough beans for them to fit snug in pepper rings.

Variation: You may make "Carrots in Bell Pepper Rings" using small red or green peppers cut into eight 1/2" rings and 2 pounds carrots scraped and cut into long uniform 1/4" thick strips. Divide carrots into eight equal bunches and slip into pepper rings. Place in shallow container of ice water; refrigerate. Drain well and serve.

Note: You may use as garnish around roasts, turkey or ham.

TOMATO/CHEESE GRITS

1 16-oz. bx. yellow or white grits,
   cooked according to directions
*2 #2 cans stewed tomatoes, chopped
1 lb. extra sharp Cheddar cheese
   (grated)

1 stick butter
2 T. sugar
1 tsp. Tabasco sauce (or more if
   you like it hot)

Drain tomatoes; reserve liquid. In a large pot, cook grits according to package directions (using tomato liquid for part of water). During last few minutes of cooking, stir in chopped tomatoes, cheese, butter, sugar and Tabasco sauce. Serves a crowd.

Wonderful with fried fish and fried canned biscuits.

*Crushed tomatoes may be substituted.

VELVET GRITS

6 C. boiling water
1 1/2 C. uncooked grits
2 tsp. salt
1 lb. Velveeta cheese, cut in fourths

1 1/2 sticks margarine
3 eggs, beaten
1 T. Tabasco sauce

Boil grits in water and salt for 5 minutes. Add cheese and butter. Remove from heat; cover and cool, stirring occasionally. Add beaten eggs and Tabasco sauce. Pour into greased 9x13" casserole dish. Bake at 350° for 1 hour. Makes 8 to 10 servings.

Note: Tastes like velvet feels.

FESTIVE ENGLISH PEAS

2 15-oz. cans LeSueur English peas
1 sm. jar pimiento, chopped

1/2 C. pearl onions
1 tsp. butter or margarine

Combine ingredients in a saucepan. Heat and serve.

EASY HASH BROWN POTATO CASSEROLE

1 32-oz. pkg. frozen
   hash brown potatoes
1 med. onion, chopped
1 can cream of chicken soup

1 8-oz. ctn. dairy sour cream
1/2 C. Parmesan cheese, grated
Paprika, to garnish

Place hash browns evenly in bottom of 9x13" casserole dish. In a bowl, stir together onions, soup and sour cream. Pour over hash browns. Sprinkle Parmesan cheese on top. Garnish with a little paprika. Makes 8 to 10 servings.

POTATO ROSES

3 C. hot, boiled white potatoes,
   riced or mashed
3 T. butter or margarine
1 tsp. salt

3 egg yolks, beaten
Hot milk*
1 egg, beaten
1 T. milk

*Enough to thin mixture so it will pass through rose tip of pastry bag.

Mix potatoes, butter, salt and beaten egg yolks. Add just enough to make mixture soft enough for use in pastry bag. To shape roses, put rose tip on pastry bag. Butter a cookie sheet. Fill bag with potato mixture. Hold the bag upright with tube downward. Guide tube with left hand and press out potato mixture onto cookie sheet with the right (reverse if you're left-handed), making a circular motion. When roses are desired size, press the tube gently into mixture and pull it out quickly. Brush each rose with 1 egg mixed with 1 tablespoon milk. Brown in a 300° oven.

Very pretty placed around a roast or ham.

Note: Sweet potatoes may be used if you prefer.

BAKED WILD RICE

1 C. wild rice, washed, drained
1 can beef consomme
1/2 C. water

1/2 lb. fresh mushrooms, sliced
1 T. butter or margarine

Place washed rice in 9x13" casserole dish; add consomme and water. Let stand, covered, for 3 hours at room temperature. Then bake, covered, for 45 minutes at 350°. Uncover, add mushrooms that have been sauteed in 2 tablespoons butter. Fluff rice with a fork and bake, uncovered, at 300° until all liquid is absorbed. Serves 4.

CHARLESTON CHRISTMAS RICE

2 C. cooked white rice
1/4 C. green pepper, diced
1/4 C. pimiento, diced

1/2 C. mushroom pieces, drained
1 T. chicken broth or 1 T. butter

In a heavy saucepan, simmer all ingredients together for 5 minutes or until heated through. Stir once or twice. Serve immediately. Makes 4 servings.

Good with meat, poultry or seafood.

Note: Double ingredients to serve 8.

Add 1 tablespoon white vinegar to rice just as it begins to boil. Rice will be light and fluffy.

When frying onion rings or green tomatoes (or any vegetable), dip into ice water first, then follow your recipe. This makes them very crisp.

. . . hearts go home for the holidays

SPINACH CASSEROLE

3 10-oz. pkg. frozen chopped spinach
2 3-oz. pkg. cream cheese, softened
   and cut in 6 pieces
4 T. butter or margarine, melted
1 tsp. Tabasco sauce

Salt and pepper, to taste
Dash nutmeg
1 tsp. celery salt
Grated rind of 1 lemon
1 6-oz. pkg. herb stuffing

In a saucepan, cook spinach as directed on packages; drain and return to pan. Add cream cheese and 2 tablespoons melted butter. Add Tabasco sauce, salt, pepper, nutmeg, celery salt and grated lemon rind. Pour into a buttered 9x13" casserole dish. Sprinkle dry stuffing on top and pour remaining melted butter evenly over stuffing. Bake at 350° for 25 to 30 minutes. Makes 8 to 10 servings.

Note: This can be made in individual small baking dishes (ramekins). Just divide evenly among them and follow same directions.

BAKED TOMATO CASSEROLE

2 16-oz. cans stewed tomatoes
1/4 C. butter or margarine
1 med. onion, chopped
1 med. bell pepper, chopped
2 C. day old bread crumbs

1 tsp. salt
1/2 tsp. basil
1/4 tsp. pepper
4 tsp. sugar

Cook onion and bell pepper in butter or margarine until tender (about 5 minutes). Add all of the remaining ingredients. Mix. Place in casserole dish. Top with buttered bread crumbs. Bake in 375° oven for 30 minutes or until hot and bubbly. Serves 6.

For topping: Use 1 to 2 cups bread crumbs mixed with soft butter or margarine. Grated cheese may also be used if desired.

STEAMED VEGETABLE DISH

1 bunch broccoli
1 head cauliflower

1 bunch fresh asparagus
Butter, salt and pepper, to taste

Wash vegetables. Remove tough stem parts of broccoli. Trim ends of asparagus. Remove outer leaves of cauliflower (keeping head intact). Place in steamer basket over boiling water. Season to taste. Cover and steam for 10 minutes. Check to see if tender. Cook until preferred tenderness. Serve on a platter with Hollandaise Sauce (see Table of Contents).

Note: Do not overcook or you'll have "mush"!

"Fat" fish such as salmon, mackeral, lake trout and whitefish are best for baking and broiling. "Lean" fish such as flounder, perch, cod, haddock, bream, trout, bass and catfish are best for frying. Do not overcook.

Add a thick slice of onion to the oil when frying fish and hushpuppies. It helps to keep batter from burning and smells wonderful!

Soak canned shrimp in ice water. Drain thoroughly. The same for canned crab meat.

- MAIN DISHES -

MACARONI AND CHEESE

8 oz. elbow macaroni
1 T. plus 2 tsp. butter or margarine
1 1/2 C. sharp Cheddar cheese,
    cut in cubes
Salt and pepper, to taste
1/2 tsp. dry mustard

3 eggs
1 tall can evaporated skim milk or
    regular milk
1/2 C. sharp Cheddar cheese, grated
Paprika, to garnish

Boil macaroni in salted water (use directions on package). Drain. Stir in butter and cheese. Add salt, pepper and dry mustard. Stir. Beat eggs and milk together. Add to macaroni mixture. Stir to blend and pour into buttered 9x13" casserole dish. Top with grated cheese; garnish with paprika. Bake at 350° for 30 to 45 minutes or until set. Makes 6 to 8 servings.

CRAB MEAT STUFFED TOMATO PETALS

1 C. celery, chopped fine
1/2 C. green pepper, chopped fine
8 stuffed green olives, minced
1 (6 1/2-oz.) can crab meat*, drained
1/2 C. Hellmann's mayonnaise

1 T. lemon juice
1/2 tsp. salt
1/4 tsp. lemon pepper
4 tomatoes
Parsley sprigs, for garnish

*A 6 1/2 ounce can of tuna may be substituted.
Wash tomatoes; pat dry. Place 1 each on lettuce leaf in salad plate. Cut slice off top. Cut from top to bottom in 4 to 6 sections to resemble petals. Do not cut through bottom. With bottom of tomato intact, gently press "petal" like sections slightly outward and place equal amounts of crab mixture in each.

OYSTER WREATH CASSEROLE

2 12-oz. pkg. fresh oysters, drained
1/2 C. finely chopped green onions
1/2 C. chopped fresh parsley
1 C. plain bread crumbs
2/3 C. butter

1 T. fresh lemon juice
1/2 tsp. dry mustard
2 1/2 tsp. Worcestershire sauce
1/2 tsp. Tabasco sauce
Parsley, to garnish

Place drained oysters on a tea towel for a few minutes. Pat dry. Place oysters in a buttered round baking dish (at least 10" in diameter). Add a layer of green onions, then parsley. Top with cracker crumbs. Mix the next 5 ingredients and pour over cracker crumbs. Bake at 350° for 25 to 30 minutes. When done, arrange fresh parsley on outer edge of top to resemble a wreath.

Note: May be baked in a rectangular dish as well if wreath shape is not desired.

CHRISTMAS STIR-FRY

4 T. oil
1 lg. onion, sliced in 1/8" thick rings
1 green pepper, cut in 1" squares

1 lg. tomato, cut in 8 wedges
1 lb. shelled and deveined shrimp
 (either fresh or frozen)

In a wok or heavy skillet, heat oil. Stir-fry onion rings 1 minute, stirring constantly. Stir in peppers and shrimp. Stir-fry for 2 minutes on medium/high heat. Stir in tomatoes. Cook 1 minute more, stirring ingredients together. Serve hot. Makes 4 servings.

Red and green. Pretty on your holiday table.

If you do not have fresh or frozen shrimp, you can use canned. Place over top and stir in at the last minute.

BAKED BEEF STEW

2 lb. stew beef pieces
2 15-oz. cans tomato sauce mixed with
 3 T. butterscotch pudding mix and
 1/2 C. water
2 med. onions, sliced
8 carrots, cut in quarters

8 med. potatoes, quartered
1/2 tsp. salt
1/4 tsp. ground ginger
1/4 tsp. pepper
1/2 C. wine

Combine all ingredients. Pour into large casserole dish. Cover with foil. Bake (do not uncover) at 275° for 5 hours.

Note: This is a wonderful dish for busy days before and during the holidays. Just put in the oven and forget it for 5 hours!

BAKED CURED HAM

Wash country cured ham thoroughly and put in covered roaster, fat side up. Pour 2" of water into pan. (Wine, ginger ale, apple cider, orange juice, pineapple juice, peach pickle juice or champagne may be substituted for the water.) Roast in a moderate 350° oven approximately 20 minutes per pound or until done. Baste often. When nearly cooked, remove the rind and trim off some of the fat. Score the surface of the fat in diamond shapes and use one of the following glazes:

Cover the fat with a paste made of one generous teaspoon dry mustard and 1 tablespoon prepared mustard. Pour over ham 1 cup orange juice or pineapple juice and return to hot 450° oven. Uncover. Finish baking. Baste it frequently.

Stud the diamond shapes with cloves and cover with brown sugar and honey. Add apple cider. Glaze in hot 450° oven, basting frequently.

Pour 8 ounces wine over ham and spread with dark molasses. Glaze in hot 450° oven for 8 to 10 minutes. Baste gently and frequently.

Serves 18 to 20.

Note: If you like your ham mild, soak in cool water for 12 hours depending on age of ham.

A festive garnish for your Christmas ham is to place spiced apple rings in a bed of parsley around the ham. Then place red and white small candy canes in the hole of the spiced apple ring. Makes a beautiful presentation.

CHRISTMAS MORNING CASSEROLE (BREAKFAST OR BRUNCH)

2 lb. hot bulk sausage (Jimmy Dean)
8 slices bread, crusts removed
3/4 lb. grated sharp Cheddar cheese
8 lg. eggs, beaten

3 C. milk
1 1/2 tsp. salt
1 1/2 tsp. dry mustard

In a large skillet, brown sausage; crumble and drain. Butter a 9x13" casserole dish. Place bread (torn into bite-size pieces) in bottom. Place sausage on top of bread. Sprinkle cheese over top. In a large bowl, mix beaten eggs, milk, salt and mustard. Blend well. Pour over other ingredients. Cover and refrigerate overnight. The next morning, bake at 350° for 45 minutes, uncovered. Slice in squares and serve hot. Serves 8 to 10.

Note: Breakfast cooks by itself while the gifts are being opened. Your family will love it!

This dish is very good with Tomato Cheese Grits and hot buttered biscuits.

ROASTED PORK TENDERLOIN

1 (4 to 6-lb.) boneless, whole
   pork tenderloin
1 1/2 tsp. salt

1 T. dried rosemary leaves
1 1/2 tsp. ground black pepper
Frosted grapes, for garnish

Place tenderloin, fat side up, in an open pan. Score any fat with sharp knife. In a small bowl, combine salt, rosemary and pepper. Mash slightly with back of spoon. Rub liberally on tenderloin. Roast in a preheated 325° oven for 2 to 3 hours or until done (160° on meat thermometer). Slice and serve.

Frosted Grapes:
1 lg. bunch seedless white grapes
1 egg white, beaten slightly

3/4 C. sugar, granulated

Wash grapes; pat dry. Break into smaller bunches. Dip first into egg white, then roll in sugar to coat. Let dry on wax paper. Refrigerate. When ready to serve, arrange around tenderloin.

Note: You may use 1/2 red grapes and 1/2 white.

Beef or pork roasts carve more easily if they are allowed to stand after cooking for 20 minutes. This also allows the juices to be distributed evenly.

To make meat balls uniform in size, roll ground beef out into a rectangle, then cut into equal amounts. Add seasonings and roll into balls. Try baking them instead of frying them.

Never use water when cooking wild game. It brings out the wild taste. Use butter, sliced lemon or port wine instead and dry roast.

SEAFOOD SAUCES

Cucumber Dill Sauce:

3/4 C. plain low-fat yogurt
1/2 C. unpeeled minced cucumber
1/4 C. Hellmann's mayonnaise
1 T. finely minced green onion

1 tsp. chopped parsley (fresh) or
   1/2 tsp. dried
1/4 tsp. dillweed
1/8 tsp. salt

Combine ingredients in order listed; mix well. Cover and refrigerate for 1 hour. Makes 1 1/2 cups.
Good with salmon or other fish.

Lemon/Garlic Sauce:

2 cloves garlic, peeled and
   finely minced
1 tsp. salt
1/2 C. vegetable oil
1 C. lemon juice

1 tsp. lemon zest
1 med. onion, grated
1 tsp. thyme
1/2 tsp. pepper

Mix all ingredients together by hand or in a food processor or blender. Makes 1 1/2 cups.
Serve with any seafood or dishes containing seafood.

- DESSERTS -

JILL'S MOTHER'S FRUITCAKE

Jill Patten McCurry - Alpharetta, GA
(Wife of Pierce McCurry - One of the Twelve)

3 pkg. pitted dates, cut up
1 lb. pineapple (crystals)
1 lb. cherries (crystals)
8 C. pecan halves (2 lb.), added last
2 tsp. baking powder

1/2 tsp. salt
4 eggs
1 C. sugar
1 tsp. vanilla
2 C. plain flour, sifted

Mix pineapple, dates and cherries. Sift flour together with baking powder and salt. Mix with fruit. Beat eggs and gradually beat in sugar and vanilla. Combine with fruit. Add pecans. Pack in 2 loaf pans which have been greased and lined with wax paper on bottom and lightly floured. Cook at 275° for 2 hours.

Sift flour once before measuring. Fill cup without packing.

Fresh pineapple can be peeled, sliced or cubed and frozen for later use.

REFRIGERATOR FRUITCAKE

Beatrice McCurry Miller - Charleston, SC
(One of the Twelve)

1/4 lb. candied red cherries, chopped
1/4 lb. candied green cherries, chopped
1/2 lb. pecans, chopped
1/2 lb. dates, chopped

1/2 lb. candied pineapple, chopped
1 can sweetened condensed milk
1 (13 1/2-oz.) bx. vanilla wafers, crushed*

*This is equal to 1 9-ounce box and 1/2 of another one.

This needs to be made 2 days before serving.

Combine chopped fruits and nuts with very finely crushed vanilla wafers and the condensed milk (you'll need a large bowl). Mix well. Divide mixture in half and roll into equal rolls 10" long and 2" thick. Wrap each roll in plastic wrap and then foil. Refrigerate for 2 days before serving. Slice about 1/2" thick. Serve with whipped cream.

FRUITCAKE LOAVES

1 lb. Brazil nuts or pecans
1 lb. walnuts
1 lb. pitted dates
1 1/2 C. white sugar
1 1/2 C. flour

1 tsp. baking powder
4 lg. eggs
1 8-oz. jar maraschino cherries, drained

Put nuts and dates in bowl. Sift dry ingredients into bowl; stir. Add unbeaten eggs and stir. Add cherries and mix lightly. Turn into 2 greased loaf pans. Bake at 300° for 1 hour. Yield: 2 loaves.

MERRY CHERRY PIES

1 16-oz. can sweetened condensed milk
1/4 C. lemon juice
1 16-oz. can sweet or sour cherries, drained and chopped

1 C. pecans, chopped
1 9-oz. ctn. Cool Whip
2 9" graham cracker crusts
Maraschino cherries, garnish
Sprigs of mint

In a mixing bowl, combine milk and lemon juice. Stir to blend. Add drained cherries, nuts and Cool Whip. Blend together well. Pour into pie crusts. Chill 4 to 6 hours or overnight. Garnish with maraschino cherries and sprigs of mint.

PECAN PIE

3 eggs, beaten until frothy
1 C. light brown sugar, packed
1 C. light corn syrup
1/8 tsp. salt

1 C. chopped pecans
3 T. butter, melted
1 9" unbaked pie shell

In a bowl, beat eggs with a fork or whisk until frothy. Add sugar, a little at a time. Pour in syrup and remaining ingredients. Mix well. Pour into unbaked pie shell. Bake in a preheated 350° oven for 45 to 50 minutes. Cool. Slice and serve with whipped cream or ice cream.

(ALMOND) JOY TO THE WORLD CANDY

Candy:
2 14-oz. pkg. coconut
1 1-lb. bx. confectioner's sugar
4 C. chopped almonds

1 stick margarine, melted
1 can sweetened condensed milk

Combine coconut, sugar, nuts, margarine and milk. Mix well; spread into 13x9" buttered pan. Refrigerate 10 to 12 hours. Cut into small bite-sized squares. With a toothpick, dip candy squares into chocolate Coating. Place candy on wax paper until chocolate has hardened. Makes approximately 9 pounds.

Coating:
1 12-oz. pkg. chocolate chips

1 sm. block household paraffin

Melt ingredients together.
Note: Pecans may be substituted for the almonds.

CHOCOLATE ALMOND TRUFFLES

4 C. powdered sugar
1 8-oz. pkg. cream cheese
5 1-oz. squares unsweetened
    chocolate, melted

1 tsp. vanilla
Chopped toasted almonds
Cocoa

Slowly add powdered sugar to cream cheese, mixing well after each addition. Add chocolate and vanilla; mix well. Chill several hours. Shape into 1" balls. Roll in almonds, cocoa or additional powdered sugar. Chill. Makes 48.
Note: These are pretty when served in miniature, decorative cupcake papers.

STUFFED DATES

3 C. granulated sugar
Juice of 1 lemon

1 C. nuts, chopped fine
2 bx. pitted dates

Mix sugar, lemon juice and nuts together. Stuff each date; press opening together. Roll in additional sugar. These keep for 6 to 8 weeks. Roll in more sugar every week or so.

HOLIDAY DIVINITY

2 1/2 C. sugar
1/2 C. light corn syrup
2 egg whites
1/4 tsp. salt

1 3-oz. pkg. raspberry flavored gelatin
2 tsp. vanilla extract
1/2 C. coarsely chopped walnuts
1/2 C. flaked coconut

In 1-quart heavy saucepan, combine sugar and corn syrup with 1/2 cup water. Over low heat, cook, stirring, until sugar is dissolved. Cover; cook 1 minute or until sugar crystals on side of pan melt. Remove cover; bring to boiling, without stirring; cook to 238° on candy thermometer or until a small amount in cold water forms a soft ball. Meanwhile, in large bowl of electric mixer, at high speed, beat egg whites with salt and gelatin until stiff peaks form when beater is slowly raised. In a thin stream, pour half of hot syrup over egg whites, beating constantly at high speed, until stiff peaks form when beater is raised. Continue cooking rest of syrup to 256° on candy thermometer or until a small amount in cold water forms a hard ball. In a thin stream, pour hot syrup into meringue mixture, beating constantly with wooden spoon. Beat in vanilla, walnuts, and coconut. Continue beating until mixture is stiff enough to hold its shape. Turn into a lightly greased 11x7x1¼" baking pan; spread evenly in pan. Let stand until firm. With sharp knife, cut into approximately 24 pieces.

Note: Divinity may also be dropped by teaspoonfuls onto wax paper for individual pieces. Allow to stand until firm.

WHITE FUDGE

3 tsp. cornstarch
3 C. sugar
1 C. sour cream
1/3 C. light corn syrup

1/4 tsp. salt
2 T. butter
2 tsp. vanilla
1 1/2 C. chopped nuts

Combine sugar, sour cream, syrup, salt and butter in a 2-quart saucepan. Stir until sugar is dissolved and mixture boils. Cook; reduce heat and cook 5 minutes. Uncover and boil rapidly to soft ball stage. Beat. Add vanilla and nuts. Pour into buttered dish. Cool and cut into squares.

PEPPERMINT THUMBPRINTS

1 lb. confectioner's sugar
1 egg white, beaten stiff

1/4 tsp. peppermint extract (or more)
Semi-sweet Baker's chocolate

Sift powdered sugar into a stiffly beaten egg white. Add peppermint extract (to taste, start with 1/4 teaspoon). Roll dough into small balls. Place on plate lined with wax paper; press each one flat with your thumb. Let dry at room temperature. Melt a small amount of chocolate and place a small amount on each mint. When chocolate has hardened and mints are dry, place in airtight container.

. . . hearts go home for the holidays

QUICK PRALINES

1 sm. pkg. butterscotch pudding (dry)
1 C. granulated sugar
1 C. light brown sugar

1/2 C. evaporated milk
1 T. butter or margarine
1 C. pecans

In a saucepan or heavy iron skillet, combine all ingredients except pecans and cook over low heat until sugar is dissolved. Then boil until mixture reaches soft ball stage. Add pecans. Stir until it just barely begins to harden. This hardens very quickly, so drop immediately by teaspoonfuls into 2" praline patties on wax paper. Let cool until firm. Remove to covered tins or jars.

PULLED CANDY
Pierce McCurry - Alpharetta, GA
(One of the Twelve)

2 C. light Karo
2 C. sugar
1 T. vinegar

1/4 stick butter
Capful vanilla or other flavorings
    (peppermint, chocolate, lemon)

Cook to 254° on candy thermometer. Pour in large plate (or several); let cool. Then pull with buttered hands until it turns white. Lay out like rope on buttered counter top. Cut into small pieces and wrap in wax paper.

SUGAR PLUMS

1/2 C. dried apricots
1/2 C. chopped pecans
1/4 C. dried figs or dates
1/4 C. golden raisins

1/4 C. flaked coconut
3 T. orange liqueur
1/4 tsp almond flavoring
1/4 C. granulated sugar

In a food processor or by hand, finely chop apricots, pecans, figs, raisins and coconut. Add liqueur and almond flavoring. Stir until blended. Roll into 36 balls about 1" each by placing small amount of mixture between palms of your hands. Roll each ball in granulated sugar. Store in refrigerator in an airtight container. Place a layer of wax paper or plastic wrap between each layer to prevent sticking. Serve on a glass plate lined with a paper doily. Makes 3 dozen.

TURTLE TASTIES

5 C. pecans, coarsely chopped,
    toasted

1 pkg. Kraft caramels
1 12-oz. pkg. chocolate chips

Toast pecans for 30 minutes at 250°. While pecans are toasting, melt caramels in a heavy saucepan (or microwave). Mix pecans into caramels. Cool. Melt chocolate chips and pour into cooled mixture. Drop by teaspoonfuls onto buttered cookie sheets. Cool.

CHARLESTON SANDIES

1 1/2 sticks margarine	2 C. plain flour
5 T. powdered sugar	1 C. nuts, chopped
1 T. ice water	1 tsp. vanilla
Pinch of salt	

Cream margarine, sugar and other ingredients. Shape into rounds (flatten) or roll in crescents. Bake on cookie sheet at 250° for 40 minutes. Dust or roll in powdered sugar. Makes about 80.

Dough will be stiff, so shape into roll to make it stick together before making shapes.

Also know as Wedding Cookies or Moldy Mice Cookies.

CHRISTMAS SHORTBREAD

3/4 C. all-purpose flour	1/4 tsp. aniseed, chopped
1/3 C. granulated sugar	1 stick unsalted butter
1/4 C. cornstarch	Ice cream

Melt butter and cool. Preheat oven to 325°. Mix flour, sugar, cornstarch and aniseed. Pour butter over mixture and stir well. Place dough in bottom of a 9" pie plate and spread evenly. Pierce with fork to form design of a Christmas tree or wreath in center. Bake for 30 minutes. Cut while hot in 8 wedges. Top with a scoop of ice cream.

POTATO CHIP COOKIES

1 C. butter or margarine, softened	1/2 C. chopped nuts
1 C. light brown sugar	2 C. crushed potato chips
1 C. granulated sugar	2 C. flour
2 eggs, beaten	1 tsp. baking soda
1 6-oz. pkg. chocolate chips	

Sift flour and soda together and set aside. Cream butter and sugar. Add beaten eggs. Stir well. Fold in remaining ingredients until smooth. Chill dough for 1 hour, then form into 3/4" balls. Place 2" apart on lightly greased baking sheet. Bake at 350° for 10 to 12 minutes or until lightly browned. Cool on baking sheet for about 45 seconds and remove to wire rack. When completely cool, place in airtight container. Makes 7 dozen.

Keeps about 2 weeks.

PRESSED HOLLY WREATH

1/2 C. shortening	1/2 tsp. vanilla
1/2 pkg. (3-oz.) cream cheese	1 C. sifted plain flour
1/4 C. sugar	

Mix all ingredients. Use cookie press with star design and press cookies into a circle pattern. Decorate with bits of candied cherries (green or red). Bake in a moderate 375° oven only until set, not brown. Let cool slightly and remove from cookie sheet. Makes 3 to 4 dozen.

. . . hearts go home for the holidays

STAINED GLASS COOKIES

1 C. sugar
1/2 C. shortening
1/4 C. butter or margarine, softened
1 tsp. vanilla
2 eggs, beaten

2 1/2 C. plain flour
1 tsp. baking powder
1 tsp. salt
5 rolls assorted flavor "Life Savers"
    hard candy

In a mixing bowl, combine sugar, shortening, butter, vanilla and eggs. Sift flour, baking powder and salt together. Add to first mixture. Stir well. Cover with foil or plastic wrap and chill for 1½ hours. Roll dough to 1/8" thickness on lightly floured surface. Cut with 3" cookie cutters, round or any design desired. Place on a foil lined cookie sheet. With smaller cookie cutters, cut shapes from each cookie. Fill "holes" with hard candy, broken into several (2 or 3) pieces each (place in a Ziploc bag and hit lightly with wooden kitchen mallet or rolling pin). Bake in a preheated 375° oven for 8 to 10 minutes. Cool 30 minutes on cookie sheet before removing cookies. Makes approximately 72 cookies.

May be used as tree ornaments if you cut a hole about 1/4" from top of each cookie before baking. Hang with ribbon or twine.

Note: Twine may be colored by dipping in food coloring and water and allowed to dry.

VERSATILE SUGAR COOKIES

1 C. soft butter
1 1/2 C. confectioner's sugar
1 egg, beaten

1 tsp. vanilla
1 tsp. almond extract
2 1/2 C. self-rising flour

Combine butter, sugar, beaten egg, vanilla and almond extract. Mix well. Add flour gradually. Chill for 3 hours. Pinch dough into 2 pieces, roll each half 1/8" thick on lightly floured flat surface. Cut with cookie cutters. Paint if desired with Egg Yolk Paint. Bake at 375° for 7 to 8 minutes. Yield: Approximately 4 dozen.

Egg Yolk Paint:
1 egg yolk
1 tsp. water

Food coloring

Mix together.

Note: Use cookie cutters of appropriate holiday. Decorate with Egg Yolk Paint, icing or colored candies.

Scissors are a great time saver in cutting dried fruits and marshmallows.

Eggs keep longer in the carton when refrigerated

"RUBY'S"
Ruby McCurry Matthews - Lincolnton, GA
(One of the Twelve)

2 sticks margarine
1 C. light brown sugar
3 eggs, beaten
3 C. plain flour
1 tsp. cinnamon
1/2 C. buttermilk
1/2 tsp. baking soda

1 lb. candied cherries (red and green)
1 lb. candied pineapple
1 bx. dates
1 lb. raisins
1 1/2 oz. bot. sherry flavoring
7 C. nuts, chopped

Chop fruit in small pieces. Pour sherry flavoring over fruit. Let stand overnight (covered). The next day in a very large bowl, cream margarine and sugar. Add eggs. Take out 1/4 cup of flour and mix with fruit. Set aside. Add remaining flour to butter mixture a little at a time. Add cinnamon. Mix buttermilk with soda. Add to mixture. Mix well. Add fruit. Stir to blend. Drop by teaspoonfuls onto ungreased cookie sheet. Bake at 250° for 20 or 25 minutes. Makes 12 dozen.

BETTY'S CHINESE CHEWS
Betty Miller Wilkins - Prosperity, SC

1 bx. light brown sugar
1 stick margarine, softened
3 eggs, beaten

1 1/2 C. self-rising flour
1/4 tsp. vanilla
1 1/2 C. chopped nuts

Preheat oven to 350°. Combine first 4 ingredients in a mixing bowl. Add vanilla and stir in nuts. Pour into a greased and floured 9x13" baking pan. Bake at 350° for 30 minutes. Cool slightly. Cut into squares or diamonds.
Note: Dust with powdered sugar if desired.

CHOCOLATE PECAN CRUNCH BARS

18 whole graham crackers
1 14-oz. can sweetened
   condensed milk
Pinch of salt

1 6-oz. pkg. chocolate chips
   (semi-sweet)
1/2 C. chopped pecans
Powdered sugar

In a mixing bowl, crumble the graham crackers into fine crumbs. Stir in milk; add salt, chocolate chips and nuts. Pour mixture into a well-greased pan (a cookie sheet with sides works well). Bake at 350° for 15 minutes. Remove from oven. Mark into rectangular 1½x3" bars with sharp knife. When cool, cut into squares, remove from pan and roll in powdered sugar. Store in airtight container.

FRUITCAKE BARS

1 C. brown sugar
1 C. plus 1 T. plain flour
Pinch of soda
1/2 tsp. salt
1 tsp. baking powder
1 tsp. vanilla
2 eggs

2/3 stick margarine
1 C. nuts, chopped
1 pkg. dates, chopped
2 slices crystallized pineapple,
    diced in small bits
1/2 C. crystallized cherries
    (red and green), cut in half

Place fruit, nuts and dates in a bowl. Stir in 2 tablespoons flour; set aside. Cream butter and sugar; add eggs one at a time, beating after each. Sift flour, salt, soda and baking powder together. Fold into butter/egg mixture. Add vanilla. Fold in floured fruits and nuts. Spread in a jelly-roll pan or cookie sheet with sides, lined with wax paper. Bake at 300° for 45 minutes. Cool and cut into 1½x4" strips. Store in airtight container.

OATMEAL JAM BARS

1 1/3 C. all-purpose flour
1/4 tsp. baking soda
1/4 tsp. salt
3/4 C. quick-cooking rolled oats
1/3 C. packed brown sugar

1 tsp. finely shredded lemon peel
2 3-oz. pkg. cream cheese, softened
1/4 C. butter or margarine, softened
3/4 C. blackberry jam
1 tsp. lemon juice

Stir together flour, soda, and salt. Add oats, sugar, and lemon peel. In a small mixing bowl, blend cream cheese and butter or margarine; cut into dry ingredients until mixture is crumbly and evenly mixed. Reserve 1 cup of the crumb mixture; pat remaining in bottom of a greased 9x9x2" baking pan. Bake in 350° oven for 20 minutes. Meanwhile in small bowl, combine jam and lemon juice. Spread over prebaked crust. Sprinkle with the reserved crumbs. Bake for 15 minutes or until brown. Cool in pan on wire rack; cut into bars. Makes 3 dozen.

FIGGY PUDDING

2 eggs, beaten
1 C. granulated sugar
3 T. flour

1 tsp. baking powder
1 C. coarsely chopped nuts
1 C. chopped figs

In a large mixing bowl, beat eggs and sugar until frothy. Sift flour and baking power together 3 times. Add to egg mixture along with remaining ingredients. Stir well. Bake at 300° for 25 minutes in a greased shallow pan. Serve hot or cold. Garnish with whipped cream.

LEMON AND ORANGE CURDS

Lemon Curd:
1 C. granulated sugar
2 lg. eggs
2 lg. egg yolks
1/2 C. lemon juice

Peel from 1 med.-size lemon, removed
    as thinly as possible with a
    vegetable peeler
1/4 C. unsalted butter or margarine

Whisk sugar, eggs and egg yolks in a small heavy saucepan until well blended. Stir in lemon juice and peel; add butter. Cook, stirring often, over low heat about 10 minutes. As the mixture thickens, stir constantly (don't boil or mixture may curdle) 8 to 10 minutes longer until it thickly coats back of a metal spoon. Pour through a strainer set over a bowl; cover surface with plastic wrap and refrigerate at least 4 hours. Curd will thicken as it cools. Makes 1 1/2 cups.

Orange Curd:
Follow directions for Lemon Curd using the peel of 1 medium-size orange instead of the lemon peel, 1/4 cup each freshly squeezed lemon and orange juice instead of all lemon juice.

Perfect for filling small tarts or meringue shells.

Note: These Curds are easily stored in covered glass jars in refrigerator. Will keep a week or so.

CHRISTMAS PARFAIT (ICE CREAM)

1 qt. pistachio ice cream
1 qt. strawberry ice cream
Whipped cream

Chopped pistachio nuts
Strawberries (whole or sliced)

In parfait glasses, alternate scoops of pistachio and strawberry ice cream with chopped pistachio nuts between layers. Top with whipped cream and a few chopped pistachios and a strawberry or strawberry slices.

Note: Serve in parfait glass placed on a lace paper doily in a small glass plate.

FRUITCAKE ICE CREAM

1 qt. vanilla ice cream

2 C. fruitcake crumbs

Let ice cream stand at room temperature until just soft. Turn into large bowl, reserving ice cream container. Add fruitcake crumbs; stir, with rubber spatula, to mix well. Pack mixture into container. Freeze for about 3 hours or until it is firm. Makes 6 servings.

. . . hearts go home for the holidays

SHERBET PARFAIT WITH RASPBERRY SAUCE

1 qt. lime sherbet
1 qt. raspberry sherbet

Fresh raspberries

Wash raspberries in cold water; drain and refrigerate. When ready to serve, place alternating scoops of both flavors of sherbet in sherbet or parfait glasses. Sprinkle raspberries on top and pour cold Sauce over all.

Sauce:
1/2 C. sugar
1/2 C. water

1/4 C. minced crystallized ginger

In a small saucepan, combine sugar, water and ginger. Cook over medium heat until sugar has dissolved. Turn heat to high and boil 30 minutes. Refrigerate Sauce until cold.

Note: Place glasses in a small glass plate lined with lace paper doily.

Beat 1/4 teaspoon cornstarch into egg whites when sugar is added for higher meringue that won't "fall".

When beating egg whites never add sugar until whites are in soft peaks. Adding sugar too early will make the meringue tough.

CANDY MAKING CHART

CANDY TEMPERATURES

Water Test - Use 1/2 teaspoon syrup.

Candy	Temperature	Stage	Texture
	230 - 234°	Thread	Makes 2" coarse thread
Fudge, Fondant, Pralines Orange Drops, Ginger Candy	234 - 240°	Soft Ball	Makes soft ball which flattens when held between fingers
Caramels, Caramel Apples Caramel Syrup	242 - 248°	Firm Ball	Makes firm ball which holds shape. May be flattened a little.
Sea Foam Candy, Taffy Toffee, Pulled Mints Rock and Horehound Candy	250 - 268°	Hard Ball	Makes hard but pliable ball
Butterscotch, Nougats Molasses Syrup	270 - 290°	Soft Crack	Threads separate, are pliable out of water
Nut Brittle, Candy Apples Lollipops, Hard Candy	300 - 310°	Hard Crack	Separate into brittle threads

CANDY MAKING HINTS

--Let candy cool to lukewarm or 110° before beating. Less beating is required and the mixture is less likely to be grainy.

--Candy should not be placed outdoors or in a draft to cool. Place in a pan of cold water to cool quickly.

--Add a little white corn syrup to any candy recipe to prevent graining. Add 2 table-spoons of corn syrup to fudge.

--To keep candy syrup from boiling over, rub the inside of the pan with butter to within 1" of the top.

--Do not scrape pan when pouring out candy.

--Corn syrup, molasses and honey in a recipe will give finer crystals to a creamy mixture. Cook at a slightly higher temperature than for straight sugar candy.

--Creamy candy should not be overcooked. If cooked at too high of temperature, add a little water and re-cook.

--Cool creamy candy before beating. Use small amount of corn syrup or 1/3 teaspoon cream of tartar to 2 cups sugar instead of corn syrup to prevent grainy candy.

--Fresh, dried, canned, sweetened or unsweetened milk can be used in making candy. If condensed milk is used, water should be added according to directions on can.

ORDER FORM

. . . hearts go home for the holidays

(Holiday Recipes Cookbook)

Make checks payable to:
Heirlooms by Radford

Mail to:
Heirlooms by Radford
P. O. Box 517
Lincolnton, GA 30817

Name _____

Address _____

City _____ State _____ Zip _____

Please send .... copy(ies) of . . . HEARTS GO HOME FOR THE HOLIDAYS cookbook at $17.95 plus $2.00 postage and handling each (Ga residents add sales tax). Enclosed is my check or money order in the amount of $ ....

For WHOLESALE rates, call 1-800-858-1062.

ORDER FORM

Hospitality Southern Style

(Southern Recipes Cookbook)

Make checks payable to:
Heirlooms by Radford

Mail to:
Heirlooms by Radford
P. O. Box 517
Lincolnton, GA 30817

Name _____

Address _____

City _____ State _____ Zip _____

Please send .... copy(ies) of HOSPITALITY SOUTHERN STYLE cookbook at $17.95 plus $2.00 postage and handling each (Ga residents add sales tax). Enclosed is my check or money order in the amount of $ ....

For WHOLESALE rates, call 1-800-858-1062.

NOTES